How to Really Love Your Teen

How to Really Love Your Teen

ROSS CAMPBELL, M.D.

David C Cook
transforming lives together

HOW TO REALLY LOVE YOUR TEEN
Published by David C Cook
4050 Lee Vance View
Colorado Springs, CO 80918 U.S.A.

David C Cook Distribution Canada
55 Woodslee Avenue, Paris, Ontario, Canada N3L 3E5

David C Cook U.K., Kingsway Communications
Eastbourne, East Sussex BN23 6NT, England

The graphic circle C logo is a registered trademark of David C Cook.

Unless otherwise noted, all Scripture is taken from the King James Version (KJV); *The Living Bible* (TLB), © 1971, Tyndale House Publishers, Wheaton, IL 60189. Used by permission; *The Modern Language Bible: The Berkeley Version in Modern English* (MLB), © 1945, 1959, 1969 by Zondervan. Used by permission.

Library of Congress Cataloging-in-Publication Data
Campbell, Ross, 1936
How to really love your teenager / by Ross Campbell.
p. cm.
ISBN 978-0-7814-3913-8 (0-89693-067-X)
eISBN 978-1-4347-0559-4
1. Parent and teenager. 2. Parenting. 3. Adolescent psychology,
I. Title
HQ799.15.C36 1993
649'.125-dc20   92-41362
CIP

© 1981 Ross Campbell

Reprint Editor: Susan Martins Miller
Interior Designer: RJS Design

Printed in the United States of America
Second Edition 2003

45 46 47 48 49

062314

Contents

Foreword 7

Preface 9

1 Teenagers: Children in Transition 11

2 The Home 17

3 Unconditional Love 27

4 Focused Attention 35

5 Eye Contact and Physical Contact 49

6 Parental Self-Control 57

7 Teenage Anger 65

8 From Parent Control to Self-Control 83

9 Adolescent Depression 99

10 Helping Your Teenager Intellectually 109

11 Helping Your Teenager Spiritually 117

12 The Older Adolescent 131

Foreword

How to Really Love Your Teenager appeals to my sense of values, particularly since we live in a society that too often emphasizes the selfish and materialistic. This book of common sense guidelines shows how parents may more than simply coexist with a teenager—it shows how they can develop the relationship into something rewarding and enriching.

Roger and I have five children. In 1981, when I was asked to write the foreword, our eldest was a teenager and two more were on the verge of adolescence. For us, Dr. Campbell's book was not only instructive but most timely.

One of the strengths of the book is its simplicity, as it focuses on basics that can be incorporated into everyday life. I especially appreciated the sections about dealing with anger and frustration and about the need for unconditional love. And I was thankful for Dr. Campbell's reassuring message for parents as we cope with the moods and crises of our teenagers.

There is a recurring theme in the book that I heartily endorse—that as parents we should put our lives in order, physically, morally, spiritually, because we are role models for our children. If we accept Dr. Campbell's advice, I believe that we and our children will profit.

This is a book you'll want to read and then pass along to your friends.

Marianne Staubach
Dallas, Texas

Preface

Guiding a child through the teenage years is a complex venture and one most parents today have great difficulty with. In almost every respect, the adolescent situation is becoming worse year after year. Teenage suicide has increased so dramatically that it is now the second leading cause of death for people between the ages of 14 and 20. Academic achievement scores and standards have steadily gone down over the last several years. Drug abuse, juvenile crime, teenage pregnancy, sexually transmitted diseases, and feelings of despair are all statistically overwhelming.

What's wrong? The primary source of the problem usually lies with parents who do not have a balanced perspective about how to relate to their teenagers. Most parents have distorted ideas of what adolescence is and what they should expect of their young people.

Although most parents truly love their teenagers, they don't know how to convey that love in ways that make the teenagers feel loved and accepted. However, parents who really desire to give their teenagers what they need can learn to do so.

I have found that parents who put into practice the principles discussed in this book have a high degree of success in helping their teenagers develop properly and become responsible, mature, and conscientious adults.

Some of the basic material for this book is from my first book, *How to Really Love Your Child*. Since the needs of teenagers are more complex than those of younger children, it's necessary to apply the information differently.

As you integrate the ideas in this book into a solid and balanced approach for relating to your teenager, you'll be pleasantly surprised to discover how exciting and fulfilling it can be to really love your teenager.

Many case studies from my files and my memory are used in these pages for illustrative purposes. In all cases real names are not used, and circumstances have been changed enough to protect the identity of my clients.

1

Teenagers: Children in Transition

"I can't believe she did it," explained Mrs. Batten as she and Mr. Batten began to unfold their painful story in my counseling room. "She was such a good girl, always content, never gave us much trouble. I thought we were giving Debbie everything she needed—clothes, church, a good home.

"Why would she ever want to try to kill herself? How could she have taken all those pills? Does she really want to die, or is she just trying to get attention? I'm so confused. And she's gotten so hateful and sullen. I can't talk to her, and she won't talk to me. She just wants to spend time by herself in her room. And her grades have become terrible."

Mrs. Batten sat in her chair, her shoulders slumped, the sparkle missing from her usually bright eyes. As she told me more of her daughter's problems, I knew that she was as confused and lonely as Debbie. This was a typical example of the gap in understanding how to love a teenager.

"When did you notice these changes in Debbie?" I asked.

"About two or three years ago," replied Mrs. Batten. "But it was so gradual we didn't think anything was seriously wrong until fairly recently. Let's see. She's fifteen now. During the last few months of sixth grade we noticed she became bored—first with school. Her grades began falling. A teacher complained of her daydreaming and nonparticipation in class. She was very concerned about Debbie then. I wish we had listened to Mrs. Collins. She was such a fine teacher.

"Then Debbie gradually became bored with life. She gave up her favorite activities one by one and seemed to lose interest in everything, including church. She began to avoid her good friends and spend more and more time by herself. She talked less and less.

"But everything became even worse when she began seventh grade. She completely withdrew from her old standby friends and began running around with kids who were in trouble most of the time. Debbie's attitude worsened as she became more like her new friends. And they often led her into trouble—deep trouble.

"Yet we've tried almost everything," Mrs. Batten continued. "First, we spanked her. Then we began taking away her privileges and freedoms. We've grounded her. We've tried rewarding her for good behavior. We've talked to everyone we thought might be able to help us. I really believe we have tried everything. Can Debbie really be helped?"

"We're desperate," Mr. Batten interjected. "Did we do a poor job as parents? We've certainly tried hard enough. Is it inherited? Maybe physical? Should we get a sugar test or an EEG? Will vitamins or minerals help? We love Debbie, Dr. Campbell. What can be done? Is it hopeless?"

I saw Debbie after her parents left. She was a pretty girl with likable ways. Although unquestionably intelligent, she had difficulty speaking in a clear, audible way. She communicated mostly in grunts with many "uh-huhs." Debbie did not have the natural spontaneity and enthusiasm we like to see in a 15-year-old girl. She was obviously unhappy, and it was difficult to communicate with her.

However, when Debbie felt more comfortable, she spoke more freely and her eye contact improved. She stated by her behavior and in her words that she had lost interest in all she once cared for. She finally said, "Nothing really matters. No one cares about me and I don't care about anything. It doesn't matter anyway."

As the conversation continued, it became clear that Debbie was suffering from an increasingly frequent and serious adolescent problem—depression. She seldom felt content with herself or her life. For years Debbie had longed for a close, warm relationship with her parents, but during the past few months, she had gradually given up hope in this dream. More and more she turned to her peers, who she thought would accept her more lovingly; but her unhappiness deepened.

Sad to say, Debbie is typical of many adolescent girls. Debbie seemed to be happy and content during her earlier years. During those years, she was a complacent child who made few demands on her parents, teachers, or others. So no one suspected that she did not feel genuinely loved and accepted by her parents. Though she had parents who deeply loved her and cared for her, Debbie did not *feel* genuinely loved. Yes, Debbie intellectually knew of her parents' love and care for her and never would have told you that they didn't love her. But Debbie didn't have the precious and crucial *feeling* of being completely and unconditionally loved and accepted.

This situation is difficult to understand because Debbie's parents loved their daughter and looked after her needs to the best of their ability. Mr. and Mrs. Batten had attempted to carry out all that they had learned and had also followed good advice from experts. In addition, their marriage was indeed a good one. They had a stable relationship and loved each other. Each treated the other with respect.

Yet, the Battens, like many parents today, experienced real difficulty raising a teenager and understanding how to guide her effectively through the stages of her life to young adulthood. With pressures increasing every day upon the American family, it's easy to become disheartened, confused, and pessimistic. Rising rates of divorce, economic and financial crises, decreasing quality of education, and declining trust in leadership—all place emotional hardships on everyone. As parents suffer increasing physical, emotional, and spiritual strain, it becomes more and more difficult to care for our teenagers. I believe that a child, especially a teenager, pays the greatest price during these difficult times. Teenagers are the most vulnerable persons in our society, and their deepest need is love.

Debbie's parents had carried out their parental responsibility in raising their daughter to the best of their ability—but something wasn't right. Debbie didn't feel genuinely loved. Was it her parents' fault? Were they to blame? I don't believe so. Mr. and Mrs. Batten had always loved Debbie but had never known how to convey their love. As with most parents, they had a vague notion of the needs of a child—protection, shelter, food, clothes, education, guidance, love, etc. They had met essentially all these needs except unconditional love.

Teenagers Are Still Children

Teenagers are children in transition. They are not young adults. Their needs, including their emotional needs, are those of children. One of the most common mistakes parents, teachers, and others make regarding adolescents is to consider them junior adults. Many people in authority over teenagers overlook their childlike needs for feeling love and acceptance, for being taken care of, and for knowing that someone really cares for them.

Far too many teenagers today feel that no one really cares about them. As a result, many of them have feelings of worthlessness, hopelessness, helplessness, poor self-esteem, and self-deprecation.

Today's teenagers are sometimes described as the "apathetic generation." This apathy is on the surface. Beneath this surface is anger and confusion. Why is this? Because so many teens see themselves in a negative way, as unappreciated and worthless. Such a self-concept is the natural result of not feeling genuinely loved and cared for.

Two of the most frightening results of this apathy are depression and revolt against authority. Apathetic teens can become easy prey for unscrupulous persons who use young people for their own ends. They are susceptible to being influenced by authoritarian persons who themselves are anti-authority, against legitimate authority. As a result, our society is becoming increasingly angry against authority and authority figures. This is a dangerous threat in a democratic society where security rests on trust and personal responsibility. But there are ways that we will discuss later to prevent apathy in teenagers and to promote healthy, energetic, productive, and creative attitudes.

Influence of the Home

Parenting teenagers in today's world is difficult. One important reason for this is that most of a teenager's time is spent under the control and influence of others—school teachers, peers, neighbors, and television entertainers. Many people feel that regardless of how well they do their jobs as parents, their efforts have a small effect on their teenagers. But the opposite is true. Evidence indicates that the home is stronger than any other influence in determining how happy, secure, and stable teenagers are; how they relate to adults, peers, or children; how confident they are in themselves; and how they respond to new or strange situations. Regardless of the many distractions in the life of a teenager, the home has the deepest influence.

Teenagers may be bigger, smarter, stronger, or in other ways superior to their parents. But emotionally they are still children. They continue to need to feel loved and accepted by their parents. Unless teenagers feel that priceless assurance of love and acceptance by their parents, they will not be their best or do their best. They cannot reach their potential.

Relatively few teenagers are fortunate enough to feel truly loved and accepted as they should be. True, most parents have deep feelings of love toward their teenagers. They assume that they naturally and effectively convey this love. This is indeed the greatest error parents make today, for most parents are simply not transmitting or conveying their own heartfelt love to their teenagers. They don't know how!

As I work with teenagers who come to me with problems, a common, interweaving thread constantly presents itself as either the cause or the aggravator of their troubled situations—a feeling of not being loved and cared for by their parents.

That is what this book is all about. It's a how-to book to help parents know how to love their teenagers so they will be their best, act their best, and grow to become their best. I pray that it will be not only a book of answers for the weary, confused parent, but also a book of hope.

I, for one, love teenagers. They are among the dearest people I know. Given what they need emotionally, they are able to respond in such wholesome and joyful ways that sometimes I think my heart will burst.

Yes, they are definitely capable of trying us to our utter limits of tolerance and patience. Yes, sometimes we lose our cool and our tempers and feel we simply do not have what it takes to meet their needs. We may even want to run away or give up.

But hang in there! Your perseverance is indeed worth it. It's a priceless wonder to see teenagers develop into pleasant and productive adults. But we must be realistic. This doesn't just happen. We must pay a price.

I truly want this book to be a source of hope to you. The last thing I want is to cause you to feel guilty. We all make mistakes. Just as there are no perfect children, there are no perfect parents. Don't let guilt from past mistakes damage your efforts to raise your teenagers well.

Most adolescent problems can be alleviated or rectified by correcting tensions in the parent-teenager relationship. However, some teenage problems are caused or aggravated by neurological ills or physiological depression. These medical problems must be alleviated before attempting to correct parent-teenager relationships.

But most teenage problems do not require professional help. Your relationship with your teen can improve when you know how to genuinely and effectually transmit love to your teenager. And that's what this book is all about.

2

The Home

The first responsibility of parents is to provide a loving and happy home. And the most important relationship in the home is the marriage bond, which takes primacy even over the parent-child relationship. The security of a teenager and the quality of the parent-child bonding largely depend on the quality of the marital bonding. You can see how important it is to assure the best possible relationship between husband and wife since this is the basis for seriously attempting to relate to a teenager in a more positive way.

Chuck

Chuck's parents brought him to me because he had problems of truancy, stealing, and disobedience. The Hargraves talked about their teenage son with frustration and anger. The intensity of their negative feelings toward the boy concerned me.

Chuck said nothing; he sat solemnly with his eyes downcast while he listened to his parents' accusations. When he finally spoke, he did so in a soft, meek voice and with short phrases rather than sentences.

I spent some time with Chuck alone after his parents left the office. He was angry, but he couldn't tell me exactly why. It soon became evident that Chuck was a confused boy. He was confused about himself and about the relationship between his parents. He also was puzzled regarding his misconduct, for he was a bright boy who had not experienced academic problems. He was well liked by his peers and had no unusual problems with his teachers. He was also confused about his stealing since he did not need the items that he took. And it was obvious that he had set himself up to be caught.

Chuck's case is not unusual. Although his parents meant well, they had made several mistakes in raising Chuck. Their marriage was in trouble, largely because they had not learned to share their feelings and opinions with each other. Mrs. Hargrave had never been able to express her normal anger in an open, healthy, direct way to her husband; therefore, she manifested her anger by getting back at him in subtle and indirect ways—such as overspending. Mr. Hargrave, who was unable to be openly honest with his wife, expressed his anger by being silent, avoiding eye contact, and evading family and home responsibilities.

Chuck had learned his lesson well. Because open, honest discussion and expression of feelings did not exist in the Hargrave home, Chuck demonstrated his anger by doing things that embarrassed and upset his parents.

Due to lack of normal communication, Mr. and Mrs. Hargrave had never understood each other's feelings and expectations regarding Chuck. So they had never agreed on behavioral limits or appropriate discipline for their son.

This had been confusing to Chuck, for he had never known his parents' expectations of him. He was a boy who naturally wanted to please. But how could he? He gave up trying to live up to his parents' standards because he never knew what they were.

All these problems existed because the parents were never able to talk things out between themselves and come to mutual decisions.

Roger
Fourteen-year-old Roger was caught breaking into a home and stealing several items. His parents brought him to me because he was failing in school, had developed a defiant attitude, and usually was in a sullen mood. A history revealed that Roger's parents had

been having problems with him for several years. He usually dis-obeyed, constantly challenged parental authority, and would get his way by manipulation. He used what one parent said against the other. These tactics caused conflict between the parents. Mom and Dad fought about how to handle Roger, while Roger did as he pleased.

Evaluation revealed that Roger had perceptual problems, was deeply depressed, and exhibited passive-aggressive traits (see chapter 7). When I gave them my recommendations, Roger's parents, in their typical way of handling problems, argued with each other about what they should do. Even with professional recommenda-tions, these unfortunate parents were unable to come to logical and sensible decisions regarding their son.

Of course, one of my main objectives in this case was to help the parents improve their own relationship so that they would be unit-ed in the discipline of Roger. For only then would the boy respect his parents, stop using one against the other, and learn to control himself in appropriate ways.

Need for Communication

These brief case histories from my files reveal how problems in marital relationships can produce difficulties among our teenagers. Every teenager needs parents whose marital relationship is one of stability, respect, love, and good communication.

The ability to communicate feelings, particularly unpleasant feelings, is critical in marriage. Especially during times of stress, honestly, openly talking out problems is absolutely critical and can determine whether stress will enhance or break a marriage.

In my own marriage I have discovered this importance of com-munication over and over—and usually the hard way. Probably the most stressful period of our marriage was right after the birth of our second daughter, Cathy, who was born with several physical deformities. I had a difficult enough time handling this. But when she was about a year old, it slowly became apparent that Cathy was profoundly mentally retarded along with having cerebral palsy and a severe seizure disorder. As a 24-year-old husband and father, I experienced feelings that I didn't know were possible. I felt anger, rage, extreme pain, and feelings of guilt and inadequacy as a man, as a father, and as a husband. I could hardly bear it. Many times I just wanted to run, especially as we saw no improvement in Cathy's condition. She was developing no self-help skills or physical abilities.

Cathy was a childcare nightmare. When she could finally move herself along the floor, she would head straight for trouble; she would try to eat garbage or anything else she could put in her mouth. She had little sense of pain and often would attempt to place her hands on the hot stove burners. We had to watch Cathy closely every second because her constant striving was toward doing things that were dangerous to her.

All this began in my first year of medical school. With Cathy's expenses and the pressures of medical school, our financial situation was bleak. I remember wondering many times how our marriage could possibly survive.

Pat has always been the more emotionally mature partner in our marriage. The pain about Cathy and our untenable situation was just as difficult for her as it was for me. But her response was so different from mine. In the midst of constant heartbreak, Pat carefully looked after Cathy's every need with patience, gentleness, and devoted love. She seldom gave in to the agonizing feelings that were driving me away. Her inner beauty of love, gentleness, and patience were beyond my comprehension. And, worst of all, I couldn't appreciate her qualities as I should have because they contrasted with my inability to cope with the situation. I felt her maturity made me look bad as a husband and father. I somewhat resented her for this and tended to pull away from her and Cathy whenever I reasonably could.

Yet I truly loved Pat, and I realized that instead of helping her, I was adding to her crushing burden. So I felt guilty and utterly helpless. I went to several people seeking help on how to deal with this agony. But no one knew what I was talking about.

I believe things came to their absolute worst when the "patterning" method of treating children like Cathy came into vogue. It took five people to move her arms, legs, and head in coordinated movements to simulate the movements of crawling. This required our family's total resources for several hours each day. The utterly crushing consumption of time and effort came close to being the ton that broke the Campbells' backs.

Eventually we found, as did many others, that there is flimsy rationale for patterning. It turned out to be a total waste of time. But before we drew this conclusion, our family was in shambles.

Even at this point of profound gloom, Pat continued her motherly care with gentleness, love, and unbelievable patience. She had not lost her inner peace and incredible inner beauty.

Me? I was hardly coping. I hurt inside for Cathy from morning to night. I had difficulty concentrating on my studies and kept wondering how we were going to manage financially. In short, I was miserable and feared that we could not survive much longer. I wondered, "How much stress can a marital relationship bear? Will it break or simply die?"

By this time Cathy was five years old. The situation was generally the same, but her seizures were becoming worse and were less and less controlled by medication. Eventually, the slightest environmental change would set off another seizure. Cathy would not eat for three days following a seizure. When the frequency increased to several a day, forced-tube feeding became necessary. Finally, it was obvious that Cathy could not survive outside of a hospital. Then came the most difficult, agonizing decision and day of our lives—we had to place Cathy permanently in a hospital for the mentally retarded. Imagine turning our precious five-year-old daughter over to people we didn't even know. I wasn't sure I could handle this one at all. But, again, I noticed my dear, dear wife, Pat. Struggling with just as much pain and agony as I, she knew what we had to do, made the decision, found the courage to accept it, and never lost her inner peace and beauty.

Unfortunately, I learn rather slowly. But this time, instead of fighting an unchangeable situation right down to my last guilt-ridden ounce of energy (including resenting my wife's beautiful way of responding to life's most unbearable agonies), I decided that I had much to learn from her. She had taught me, as only a woman can do, how to live with life's most unbearable situations.

Every type of personality has its advantages and disadvantages. In the situation with Cathy, Pat was the stronger and I needed to learn from her, and sometimes lean on her. In other situations, I happen to be better able to cope, and then I can help Pat.

The point of all this is to understand that stress will come into every marriage. Whether the stress hurts and destroys the marriage or enhances it depends on how both husband and wife respond individually to the stress. My initial response to a cruel situation was destructive. I tended to avoid it, leaving Pat to handle the entire burden by herself. By her consistent example, she showed me how to live out my commitments as husband and father and to take my responsibility. As I did, my appreciation and love for her mushroomed. Because I learned to cope with inner pain rather than to run from it, Pat and I over the years have been able to face together problems that produce emotional pain.

Fellow parents, if we persevere through the problems that put stress on our marriages, we will grow as spouses. If we continue to carry out our marital responsibility as a lifelong commitment, we will grow together in love, appreciation, and respect. We must live and think as though there are no other alternatives than to make this marriage work. Yes, it is work. It is hard work. And it takes this lifelong commitment of both spouses. Many marriages today are based on a "wait-and-see" attitude: "We'll give it a try and if it doesn't pan out, we'll split." No marriage can truly succeed on that basis. Is there anything more rare today than total, lifelong commitment to marriage? Our way of life has been based on the integrity of the family. Yet unless it is rekindled and enhanced, the institution of marriage may be doomed.

A Look at Single-Parent Families

In 1989, 26 percent of children under 18 years of age lived with only one parent, and this figure is steadily increasing. Over 50 percent of children born today will spend at least some of their youth in a single-parent household.

Many people today believe that a single parent is incapable of being as effective in parenting as two parents raising their children together. David Clevenger's article "Parenting in the '90s," in the American Medical Association Auxiliary magazine *Facets* (September 1992), points out that those who believe single parents cannot be effective parents are wrong. Decades of research show, as Clevenger states, that "being a single parent does not preclude anyone from being an effective parent. To some degree and in some ways, personal and societal pressures diminish the ability of most people to be good parents. And those pressures stack the odds more heavily against single parents trying to raise their children alone."

The Clevenger article states that T. Berry Brazelton, M.D., one of America's best-known and highly respected pediatricians, says, "It matters a great deal if you are single or not. But I still think you can do it. It's just harder because you are likely to be poor. It is very, very hard to be single because you have to be both the disciplinarian and somebody who offers nurturance."

Also, the single parent usually must both earn the family's living and run the household. Alvin Poussaint, M.D., Harvard psychiatrist, states: "The homemaking mother took care of a lot of those things that are so important to the family. She was there when the kids came home. She got the kids ready for school. She went to the Parent-Teacher Association meetings. She took the kids to the doctor, to the dentist. Well, if you are a single parent and you are working, who does all those things? It's just a constant pressure."

In his article, David Clevenger also points out:

> In fact, the biggest cause of diminished parental energies and competencies is poverty, a factor that disproportionately affects single mothers. Today, about eight percent of America's dual-parent families live in poverty. But of the families that are headed by a mother, as a majority of single-parent families are, nearly forty-five percent struggle below the poverty line.
>
> Why do poverty and other pressures diminish the single person's parenting effectiveness more than they do that of the traditional parent? Mothers and fathers in traditional families have each other. And they usually give each other important emotional, psychological, physical, and financial support that is not typically available to the single parent who must raise her (or his) kids alone.
>
> The absence of this support may appear to be a good rea-

son to argue that the single-parent family is not a viable family structure in which to raise children. But those who make this argument miss an important point—single parents can get support too. While they can't turn to spouses, they can rely on others with whom they are involved—on members of their extended families, and on friends, professional organizations, churches, and community groups.

And this support, wherever it's obtained, is essential for overcoming the pressures that diminish effective parenting. In fact, the most successful single parents are those who have learned how to tap into available support, and use this support to overcome the pressures that would prevent their using a positive pattern of parenting. And by overcoming them, they can become effective parents.

Role Reversal

A situation rather common today is the role reversal in which a parent demands that a child fulfill the parent's emotional needs. While this can happen in any home, it's more likely to occur in a one-parent family.

Some single parents feel tempted to use their teenagers as colleagues or confidants because they do not have spouses with whom to share the adult levels of the home.

Because of loneliness, feelings of inadequacy, depression, or other causes, single parents at times find it difficult to avoid relating to their teenagers as contemporaries. These parents may share intimately personal information that the teenagers are not ready to handle. Such parents tend to be "best friends" with their teenagers instead of maintaining healthy parent-child relationships.

Jim was a 16-year-old who frequently would get drunk with his father in a bar. Although this happened because of the father's loneliness and lack of friends, the father rationalized to himself that he was "making a man" of his son. Julie's mother would have her boyfriend bring a date for Julie so they could go out together.

While these are obviously extreme examples, role reversal is not unusual. Lesser forms of misusing teenagers in this way are very common. For example, parents complain to teenage children about how lonely, depressed, unhappy, or misused they are. This is not parenting. A parent fulfills the emotional needs of a child or a teenager. For the teenager to fill the emotional needs of a parent is "reversal of roles" and is unwholesome. A teenager treated in this way cannot develop normally.

Whether single or married, parents must always maintain their positions as mother or father in the home. We are responsible to meet the emotional needs of our teenagers. If we reverse this natural course and look to them to emotionally nourish us, we will hurt them—and destroy our relationship with them. We must obtain our emotional nourishment elsewhere, not from our children.

I have never particularly enjoyed being an authority for anyone, especially for my children. As my children passed through their teenage years, I was tempted to treat them as contemporary friends, but I dared not. Yes, I was loving and friendly with them and enjoyed laughing and having fun. And on occasion, I would share appropriate personal information with them, but only for their educational benefit, not for my emotional benefit. I did not forget that I was their father and they needed my authority and direction. If I relinquished or neglected my responsibility for being the authority in the home—along with Pat, for she too had to assume her position of authority—my children would not be happy. They would feel insecure and be apt to develop poor behavior patterns. But this is a common problem today. Many parents try to somehow keep their teenagers "happy" and win their approval rather than use their rightful authority to lead their teenagers to mature behavior.

As parents, we must not use our children or teenagers as counselors, shoulders to cry on, emotional support, or colleagues. Of course, we can ask their opinion or advice on occasion, as long as we are not doing it in ways that prompt them to nourish us emotionally. We cannot ask them to make us feel better. There is no way to be consistently firm with teenagers if we depend on them for our emotional support.

As parents, our first responsibility is to make our children feel genuinely loved. Our second responsibility is to be authority figures for our children and to lovingly discipline them.

3

Unconditional Love

The basic foundation for a solid relationship with your teenager is unconditional love. Only unconditional love can prevent problems such as resentment, guilt, fear, or the insecurity of feeling unwanted. Only when your basic relationship with your teenager is built on unconditional love can you be confident in your parenting. Without this foundation, it's impossible to really understand your teenager or to know how to guide or deal with his or her behavior.

Without unconditional love, parenting is a confusing and frustrating burden. Love acts as a guiding light, showing you where you are and what to do next. When you begin with unconditional love, you can build your knowledge and expertise in guiding your teenager and filling his or her needs on a daily basis. You will also know where you are succeeding as a parent and where you are not.

You want to feel good about yourself as a parent. Many people question if this is possible. Let me assure you that it is definitely possible both to be a good parent and to feel confident that you are.

What Is Unconditional Love?
Unconditional love means loving a teenager, no matter what.

• No matter what the teenager looks like.

• No matter what the teenager's assets, liabilities, and handicaps are.

• No matter how the teenager acts.

This does not mean that you always like your teenager's behavior. Unconditional love means you love your teenager even when you detest the behavior you see.

Unconditional love is an ideal. You can't feel love for a teenager—or anyone else—100 percent of the time. But the closer you come to this goal, the more satisfied and confident you'll feel. And the more pleasant and satisfied your teenager will be.

As I look back to when my children were teenagers, there were times indeed when I didn't feel like a loving dad toward them. But I attempted to arrive at that wonderful goal of loving them unconditionally. I helped myself by trying to keep in mind the following guidelines that you'll want to consider in your relationship to your teenager:

• Teenagers are children.

• Teenagers will usually act like teenagers.

• Much of teenage behavior is unpleasant.

• If you love your teenager only when he or she pleases you (conditional love) and convey your love only during those times, your teenager will not feel genuinely loved. This, in turn, will make a teenager feel insecure, damage self-image, and actually prevent the teenager from developing more mature behavior. Therefore, parents are, without question, partially responsible for a teenager's behavioral development.

- If you love teenagers unconditionally, they will feel good about themselves and be comfortable with themselves. They will be able to control their anxiety and, in turn, their behavior as they grow into adulthood.

- If you love teenagers only when they meet your requirements or expectations, they will feel incompetent. They will believe it's fruitless to do their best because it is never enough. Insecurity, anxiety, and low self-esteem will plague them. There will be constant hindrances in emotional and behavioral growth. Again, a teenager's total growth depends a lot on the responsibility of parents.

As Pat and I tried to follow these guidelines, we prayed that our love for our teenagers would be as unconditional as we could make it. We realized that the future of our teenagers depended on this biblical foundation.

"Do You Love Me?"

Do you know what is the most important question on your teenager's mind? Without realizing it, a teenager is continually asking, "Do you love me?" It is absolutely the most important question in a teenager's life. And teenagers ask the question primarily through their behavior rather than with words.

"Do you love me?" The answer you give behaviorally to that question is absolutely critical. If you answer it no, your teenager will not be or do his or her best. You need to answer it yes, but few parents do. It's not that these parents don't love their teenagers. The problem is that most parents do not know how to answer yes; they don't know how to convey their love to their teenagers.

If you love your teenager unconditionally, he or she feels the answer is yes. If you love conditionally, your teenager is unsure and prone to anxiety. Your answer to that critical question, "Do you love me?" pretty well determines your teenager's basic attitude toward life. How crucial!

One of the main reasons most parents do not know how to convey their love to their teenagers is because teenagers, like younger children, are behaviorally oriented. Adults are primarily verbally oriented.

For example, a man away on a trip would make his wife happy by calling her and saying, "Honey, I love you." She would be on cloud nine. However, if he got his 14-year-old son on the phone and said, "I just want to say I love you," the teenager would likely shrug and perhaps say, "Yes, Dad, but why did you really call?"

See the difference? A teenager is behaviorally oriented, whereas an adult is primarily verbally oriented.

Having a warm feeling of love in your heart for your teenager is wonderful—but it's not enough! Saying "I love you" to a teenager is great, and parents should do it—but it's not enough. For teenagers to know and feel love, you must also love behaviorally; they are still primarily behaviorally oriented. Only then can teenagers feel you are answering yes to the crucial question in their hearts: "Do you love me?" Your teenager sees your love by what you say and do. But what you do carries more weight. Your teenager is far more affected by your actions than by your words.

It's also important to remember that your teenager has an emotional tank. This tank is figurative, of course, but the concept is real. Your teenager has certain emotional needs, and whether these emotional needs are met (through love, understanding, discipline, etc.) helps determine how he or she feels—whether content, angry, depressed, or joyful. Also, it strongly affects behavior—whether your teenager is obedient, disobedient, whiny, perky, playful, or withdrawn. Naturally, the fuller the tank, the more positive the feelings and the better the behavior.

At this point please stop and ponder one of the most important statements in this book: *Only when a teenager's emotional tank is full can a teenager be expected to be his or her best and do his or her best.* It's your responsibility as a parent to do all you can to keep your teenager's emotional tank full.

Love Reflectors

Think of teenagers as mirrors. They generally reflect rather than initiate love. If you give them love, they return it. If none is given, they have none to return. Unconditional love is reflected unconditionally, and conditional love is returned conditionally.

As an example of mirrored love, let's think again about Debbie, whom we met in chapter 1. The love between Debbie and her parents was an example of a conditional relationship. Unfortunately, her parents felt that they should continually prompt her to do better by withholding praise, warmth, and affection, except for truly outstanding behavior (when she made them feel proud). Otherwise, they withheld showing their love, feeling that too much approval and affection would spoil her and lessen her striving to be better. As Debbie grew older, she increasingly felt that her parents really didn't love or appreciate her in her own right, that they cared only about their own esteem as parents.

By the time Debbie was a teenager, she had learned well from her parents how to love conditionally. She behaved in a way that pleased her parents only when her parents did something special for her. Of course, with both Debbie and her parents now behaving this way, neither could convey love to the other because each was waiting for the other to do something first.

This is a typical result of conditional love. Love-giving eventually stops until another person does something very pleasing to get it going again. Everyone becomes more and more disappointed, confused, and bewildered. Eventually, depression, anger, and resentment set in. In the Battens's case, this prompted them to seek help.

Emotional Tanks

Remember, teenagers are children emotionally. Consider how a teenager is like a two-year-old. Both a teenager and a two-year-old have drives for independence and both have emotional tanks. Each will strive for independence, using the energy from the emotional tank. When the emotional tank runs dry, the teenager and the two-year-old will do the same thing—return to the parent for a refill so they can again strive for independence.

For example, suppose a mother brings her two-year-old son to a new place, such as a PTA meeting. At first the child may cling to his mother for emotional support. With a full emotional tank, the child will then begin exerting his independence by exploring. At first he may simply stand next to his mother and look around. As his emotional tank becomes empty, the child will seek his mother again for a refill with eye contact, physical contact, and focused attention. Now the child is again ready to try his independence. This time he may get to the end of the row of seats before running out of emotional gasoline. Or he may interact with another person sitting nearby before his emotional tank runs dry.

Do you see the pattern? Children must repeatedly return to their parents to have their emotional tanks refilled in order to continue the quest for independence. This is exactly what happens with the teenager, especially the early adolescent. The teenager may use different means of exerting the drive for independence (and sometimes in disturbing or upsetting ways). Teenagers need the energy from their emotional tanks to do this. And where do they get their emotional tank refilled? Right! From their parents. Teenagers will strive for independence in typical adolescent ways—doing things by themselves, going places without family, testing parental rules. But they will eventually run out of emotional gasoline and come back to the parents for emotional maintenance—for a refill. This is what we want. We want our adolescents to be able to come to us for emotional maintenance when they need it.

There are several reasons why this refilling is so important:

- Teenagers need an ample amount of emotional nurturing if they are to function at their best and grow to be their best.

- They desperately need full emotional tanks in order to feel the security and self-confidence they must have to cope with peer pressure and other demands of adolescent society. Without this confidence, teenagers tend to succumb to peer pressure and experience difficulty in upholding wholesome, ethical values.

- The emotional refilling is crucial because while it is taking place, it's possible to keep open lines of communication between parents and teenagers. When a teenager's tank is empty and he or she seeks parental love, communication is so much easier.

Most parents don't realize how important it is for their teenagers to be able to come to them to have their emotional tanks refilled. During times when teenagers are striving for independence, they may upset their parent to such an extent that parents overreact emotionally and usually with excessive anger.

This emotional overreaction, if too excessive or frequent, makes it extremely difficult, and perhaps impossible, for teenagers to return to parents for emotional refills. Then, if parent-child communication is broken, teenagers may turn to peers for emotional nurturing. What a dangerous, and frequently disastrous, situation this is! For the teenager will then be easily susceptible to peer pressure, to influences of religious cults, and to unscrupulous persons who use young people.

When your teenager tests you by striving through inappropriate behavior to be independent, be careful not to overreact emotionally. This does not mean condoning the misbehavior. Express your feelings honestly but appropriately; that is, without extreme anger, yelling, name-calling, attacking the child verbally, or otherwise losing control of yourself. Look at it this way. If someone you know overreacts with a temper tantrum, how does that affect your feelings toward that person? Your respect for that person lessens, especially if he or she loses self-control often.

The more a parent loses self-control in a teenager's presence, the less respect a teenager will feel for the parent. Make every effort to maintain emotional control of yourself, regardless of how your teenager expresses the drive for independence. Keep open the avenues over which your teenager returns to you to have the emotional tank refilled. This is crucial if your teenager is to enter adulthood as a whole person.

4

Focused Attention

Giving focused attention to your teenager involves much more than providing eye or physical contact. Eye contact and physical contact, which we will discuss in chapter 5, seldom require real sacrifice by parents. Focused attention does. It requires time—and sometimes a lot of it. It may mean giving your teenager focused attention when you would rather do something else. Sometimes a teenager desperately needs focused attention when parents least feel like giving it.

Focused attention means giving teenagers full, undivided attention in such a way that they feel truly loved, that they know they are so valuable in their own right that they warrant your watchfulness, appreciation, and uncompromising regard. Focused attention makes your teenager feel that he or she is the most important person in the world to you as parents.

In the Scriptures we see a very high regard for children. King David called them the heritage of the Lord. Christ said that no one should prevent the little ones from coming to him and warned that those who offend his little ones would be better off dead. He said that unless we become as children before him, we will not enter the kingdom of God. (See Ps. 127:3–5; Matt. 18:1–10; Mark 10:13–16.)

Teenagers ought to be made to feel that they are special. Few teenagers feel this way, but, oh, the difference it makes in them when they know they are special. Only focused attention can tell them this. It's so vital to the development of their self-esteem. And it profoundly affects their ability to relate to and to love others.

I believe that focused attention is the greatest need a teenager has. Most parents have real difficulty recognizing this need, much less fulfilling it. There are many reasons for this. For example, other things they do for their teenagers—favors, gifts, and granting unusual requests—seem to substitute for focused attention at the time. These things may be good, but it is a serious mistake to use them to replace genuine focused attention. This substitution is tempting to parents because favors and gifts are easier to give and take much less time. But teenagers do not do their best, do not feel their best, and do not behave their best unless they receive that precious commodity—focused attention from their parents.

Priorities

It's not possible for me to take care of every obligation and responsibility in my life in the way I would like to. There just isn't the time. So what can I do about this? There is only one answer, and it isn't simple: I must determine my priorities, set my goals, and plan my time to accomplish them. I must control my time in order to take care of the important things first.

What are the priorities in your life? Where do your children fit into them? Do they take first priority? Second? Third? You must determine this. Otherwise, your children will take a low priority and suffer from some degree of neglect. No one else can decide for you what is important in your life.

Because life is so unpredictable, you cannot count on unlimited opportunities for nurturing your children. Therefore, you must take advantage of opportunities that you plan or that present themselves through your teenager's need. These opportunities will be fewer than you think; children are teenagers for such a short time.

Necessity of Focused Attention

Focused attention is not something that is simply nice to give if time permits. It's a critical need all teenagers have. How they view themselves and how they are accepted by the world is determined primarily by the way parents meet this need. Without focused attention teenagers experience increased anxiety because they feel everything else is more important to their parents than they are. They are consequently less secure and become impaired in their emotional and psychological growth.

Such teenagers can be identified rather easily. They are generally less mature or sure of themselves than teens whose parents have taken the time to fill their need for focused attention. These unfortunate teenagers are often withdrawn and have difficulty with peers. They are less able to cope and usually react poorly in conflict. They are overly dependent on others, including peers, and more subject to peer pressure.

Some young teenagers, however, especially girls deprived of focused attention from their fathers, seem to react in just the opposite way. They are quite talkative, manipulative, dramatic, and often seductive. They are sometimes considered precocious, outgoing, and mature as children. But as they grow older, this behavior pattern does not mature and gradually becomes more inappropriate. By the time they are older teenagers, they are usually obnoxious to their peers as well as to adults. However, even at this late date, focused attention, especially from their fathers, can go a long way in reducing their self-defeating behavior, decreasing their anxiety, and freeing them to resume their maturational growth.

How Do You Give Focused Attention?

I have found that the best way to give teenagers focused attention is to set aside time to spend with them alone. You may already be thinking how difficult that is to do. And you're right. Finding time to be alone with a teenager, free from other distractions, is what I consider to be the most difficult aspect of parenting teenagers. But let's face it—good parenting takes time. Finding time in our hyperactive society is hard, especially when teenagers have other interests parents must compete with. But this points all the more to the fact that focused attention is crucial. Today teenagers are more influenced by forces outside the family than ever before.

It takes tremendous effort to pry time from busy schedules; but when you do, the rewards are great. It's a wonderful thing to see your teenager happy, secure, well-liked by peers and adults, and learning and behaving at his or her best. But such satisfaction does not come automatically. As parents you must pay a price for it. You must find time to spend time alone with each child.

Time is difficult to manage. I tried to conserve as much time as possible for my children when they were growing up. For example, when my daughter Carey was taking music lessons near my office on Monday afternoons, I would schedule my appointments so that I could pick her up. Then we would stop at a restaurant and have supper together. At these times, without the pressure of interruption and time schedules, I was able to give her my full attention and listen to whatever she wanted to talk about.

Only in this context of being alone without pressure can parents develop that special, indelible relationship each teenager so desperately needs to face the realities of life. A teenager treasures moments such as these and remembers them when life becomes difficult, especially during those tumultuous years of adolescent conflict.

During times of focused attention, parents can make special opportunities for eye contact and physical contact with a teenager. For during these times of focused attention, eye and physical contact have stronger meaning and impact upon a teenager's life.

Watch for unexpected opportunities to spend additional time with your teenager. For example, you may find yourself unexpectedly alone with your teenager when other family members have scattered to various activities. Take this as another opportunity to fill your child's emotional tank and prevent problems brought on by a dry tank. This time of focused attention may be quite short, but just a moment or two can do wonders.

Every moment counts, for the stakes are high. What is worse than a wayward adolescent son or daughter? What is more wonderful than a well-balanced teenager?

Yes, focused attention is time-consuming, difficult to do consistently, and many times burdensome for already exhausted parents. But focused attention is the most powerful means of keeping a teenager's emotional tank full and investing in a teenager's future.

As children grow older, these times of focus need to be lengthened. Older children need time to warm up, to let their developing defenses down, and to feel free to share their innermost thoughts, especially those that may be troubling them.

As children enter adolescence, they need more time with family, not less. It is so easy to assume that since teens are rapidly becoming more independent and seem to want more and more time away from the family, that you should spend less and less time with them. This is one of the most devastating mistakes parents make today. As their children enter and progress through adolescence, parents often use their free time in ways that meet their own pleasure needs. Every teenager I've ever known interprets this as rejection, feeling that their parents care less and less about them.

Adolescents need parental time and attention as never before. They are facing strong influences daily and, unfortunately, many of these influences are unhealthy, unwholesome, and sometimes evil. If you want your teenager to be able to cope with today's world, you must spend constructive time together—especially when your teen is going through adolescent turmoils. If you do take the time to meet these needs, your teenager will gain the confidence and personal integrity to think about the kind of values he or she will live by. Teens will develop strength to stand up against divisive influences from people who have little or no regard for them but who simply want to use them.

This may seem difficult to accomplish, especially when your child is in a difficult, noncommunicative mood so commonly seen in early to middle adolescence. One secret to remember is that the psychological defenses of moody teenagers are very high, and it takes time for them to be slowly lowered to where they are able to genuinely communicate and share with you what is really on their minds. Did you catch that magic word? *Time.*

I remember when our precious Carey was 14 years old. What a year! She was undergoing the typical transitions of early adolescence and would frequently communicate only with grunts like "uh-huh," "huh-uh," or "huh?"

During this period, I made two wonderful discoveries. First, it is useless and harmful to try to force a child to open up and talk at such a time. Although it was a real temptation to badger her with questions, I discovered this was a mistake and actually worsened the situation. Second, if I spent at least 20 to 30 minutes with Carey in a pleasant way that did not put any pressure on her to communicate, her defenses would slowly come down and we were then able to really share thoughts and feelings.

One of the most effective ways to accomplish that was to take her to a restaurant. I would pick the restaurant with the slowest service in town and would try to arrive during the busiest time so we could wait in a long line. I would ask the waitress to come back a couple of times—"We're not quite ready to order." I would take time eating and then order a dessert, which I normally avoid, followed by a leisurely cup of coffee.

You see, the purpose of all this was to provide a time together when Carey was under no pressure to communicate and could still be comfortable in my presence. Standing in line in a public place meets this requirement. Other examples include fishing, hunting, hiking, taking a trip (short or long), playing a game, seeing a play, listening to an orchestra. When a teenager is with his or her father or mother but under no pressure, "just being there," the defenses will gradually come down, and he or she will begin to talk—superficially at first, and then at more meaningful levels.

By the time we finished eating, Carey would be talking fairly freely and sharing, but with the conversation mostly at a superficial level—sports, teachers, schoolwork. Then I would pay the bill, and we would go to the car.

Let me interject an interesting piece of information here. When you are driving a car with your teenager as a passenger, especially if other teenagers are with you, you somehow lose your own identity and are considered as part of the car, an extension of the steering wheel. My wife and I have really appreciated this adolescent ability; it's amazing how this facilitates adolescent conversation while riding along in the car. It's likewise amazing how much we have learned during these times.

Anyway, back to Carey and me. We would get in the car and usually, during the last mile or so before getting home, she would finally talk about things that were very meaningful to her. Things like peer relationships, family relationships, peer pressure to take drugs. Of course, the conversation couldn't be completed before we drove up to the house—typical of teenagers. The reason for this is that teenagers need to feel they have a means of "escape" when revealing meaningful information. They must feel that they are in a position to leave if the parents are not responding properly to their innermost feelings. What they fear most is not disagreement but anger, ridicule, disapproval, or rejection of them on a personal level. They must feel enough in control so that if they become too uncomfortable, they can remove themselves.

This is why Carey would wait until we were near home before she would share with me what was really important to her. So the best conversations I had with Carey were at these times. Sometimes she would disguise her own conflicts by talking about or asking about another teenager who happened to have similar problems. This is a favorite way many teenagers use to talk about awkward, embarrassing, difficult-to-handle situations.

Sometimes a teenager needs to talk with a parent about a problem but has a difficult time initiating the conversation. At such times, the teenager will frequently throw out hints. These hints can take various forms. A teenager who needs to talk, but who is in a noncommunicative mood, may say something much less threatening than what he or she actually wants to talk about. For example, a teenager may start out by asking a question about homework. Perhaps a question about the day the parent had. Or maybe a comment about the day he or she had.

Parents must be alert for such unsolicited and sometimes puzzling gestures, usually a hesitant teenager's way of asking for time and for focused attention. The teenager is "feeling us out," testing us to see what kind of mood and frame of mind we are in, to see if it's safe to approach us on an issue about which he or she feels uncomfortable.

At other times, teenagers may test our receptivity, to see if we're in a good mood, by putting out what I call a "red herring," or "smoke screen." These are pieces of information designed to upset or irritate us—a perfect device to see if we can be trusted with what is really on their minds. If we overreact, especially with anger and criticism, teenagers assume we will react to their important question the same way. Again, the more self-control and calmness we display, the more open and sharing teenagers will be with us.

These moments of opportunity are priceless. If we don't notice these times and somehow close the door to our teenagers, they will feel rejected. If we are alert and detect these subtle clues, we can respond appropriately and help teenagers, as well as demonstrate conclusively that we love them and are sensitive to their needs.

I remember many such occasions when Carey was in her early teens. Most often she would select a time when she knew her mother and I were alone with the least likelihood of interruption. You can guess when this was—just as Pat and I were ready to turn off the light for a good night's sleep. Carey's younger brothers were fast asleep, so she had no competition. First, we would see the door slowly open as Carey came in and asked her mother if she could borrow something from the adjoining bathroom. After Carey got the item she asked for and was in the process of leaving, she would turn around and say to us, "Oh, by the way. . . ."

I can't overemphasize the importance of recognizing and noting these all too familiar words, "Oh, by the way," or their equivalent. Do you know what they usually really mean when a teenager says them in such a situation? A translation is something like this: "The real reason I'm here and what I really want to talk about is coming up. But first I want to know, are you in a good frame of mind to handle it? Can I trust you with this very delicate personal part of my life? Will you take it and help me, or will you use it against me? Can I trust you?"

If we don't give that focused attention at such a time, a teen will interpret the answer to those questions to be no. But if we focus our attention directly on the child, and listen intently and quietly, letting the teen control the conversation, he or she will feel it's safe to take a chance and reveal a pressing problem. Incidentally, be ready for those famous four words soon after a "red herring" or "smoke screen."

I remember that I would sometimes goof and do something like telling Carey to be sure to turn out all the lights. And I would then feel a swift kick under the covers because my wife would recognize what Carey was telling us and would know that she needed that precious commodity, focused attention. Always when we were on course, Carey continued the conversation on her own, talking initially about superficial things and gradually about items that were more and more important to her. After a while, she would be sitting at the foot of our bed. Pretty soon she would be lying across the foot of the bed, the talk pouring out. Finally, she would get to the thing that was bothering her. I remember one such time when she said, "I don't know if Jim likes me anymore. He's been so different." How difficult that was for Carey to come out with. She had to make sure the situation was safe for her to share. She had to put out her "red herrings" and "smoke screens" before she could finally reveal her problem.

Once a sensitive issue is out, it's a real temptation for parents to make light of it with a casual, seemingly flippant reply, as though it is such a trivial or easy-to-handle issue. We must take teenagers seriously, examine their problems carefully with them, and help them come to logical and sensible solutions. In this way, we not only will help them with their problems, but more importantly, will cement our love-relationship with them.

And as we help them to solve their own problems, we can also be teaching them to think logically, rationally, and sequentially. Only by learning to think clearly can a teenager develop the ability to discern right from wrong and to develop a strong value system.

Guilt and Envy

To understand the background of most teenage problems, it's important to be aware of adolescent society. Teenage society is similar to the society of chickens: both teenagers and chickens have a "pecking order," so to speak. The adolescent society is complex, but it's based primarily on popularity and acceptance. It's important to know approximately where your child is in this network of relationships because some of the most painful adolescent problems are peer-related and involve one or more of four feelings— envy, guilt, anger, and depression. We will discuss anger and depression in detail later, so right now let's consider envy and guilt.

In dealing with peers, teenagers frequently have problems that naturally make them feel guilt or envy. Unfortunately, most teenagers are not good at identifying guilt or envy within themselves and, as a result, experience them as pain (distress) or confusion.

If a teenager's problem involves a peer who is lower on the adolescent society ladder, he or she probably will feel guilt. If the encounter was with someone higher up the ladder, the feeling usually will be envy. When a conflict of interest or position arises, the teenager on the lower end, prompted by envy, will attempt to make the upper peer feel guilty.

It's important for parents to see their teenager's position in the conflict and identify the feelings the teenager is struggling with. Explaining the situation to a teenager will help him or her in several ways:

- It will enable the teenager to understand exactly what is happening and why.

- It will help the teenager determine whether he or she has done anything wrong.

- It will assist the teenager in handling this situation and others like it.

For example, if your teenager is feeling guilty, a clear understanding of the situation will usually reveal there is no blame to be laid and that the real problem is actually the other teenager's feeling of envy.

If your teenager is feeling envious, it's so helpful for him or her to be able to identify this within and to understand why. Then you will be in a position to help your teenager correct the problem—by understanding that there is no real basis for the jealousy, if this is true, or by learning how to overcome the envy if there is a basis for it.

When Carey won the Junior Miss Pageant, nearly all of her peers were genuinely excited for her and truly proud of her. But one evening, shortly afterward, Carey seemed troubled. As it turned out, an envious peer had made Carey feel guilty about winning the contest. The statement that produced the guilt was something like this: "Well, look at the big star! She sure thinks she's hot stuff!"

Carey felt miserable, typical of a teenager in this circumstance, and could not resolve her misery. Carey's mother helped her understand her feelings of guilt—that she had done nothing wrong but was simply feeling a false guilt that had no basis.

Carey's experience illustrates the frequent problem of envy and guilt in the teenage world. It's vital to the emotional development of our teenagers that we help them to identify and understand envy and guilt in themselves, and learn how to handle these emotions properly. If they are unable to they are likely to be manipulated by guilt.

Manipulation by Guilt

This is a great problem among adolescents today. The more sensitive a teenager is, the more susceptible he or she is to being manipulated by guilt. On the other hand, the less sensitive a teen is, the more apt he or she is to use this type of manipulation on others.

The maneuver is rather simple. Manipulator finds ways to make the manipulatee feel guilty if the manipulatee does not do what the manipulator wants. Of course, the classic example of this—and one of the most destructive—is the boy who attempts to induce a girl to have a sexual encounter with him with such remarks as, "If you really loved me, you would."

The parent of a sensitive teenager is in an excellent position to teach the child about this unwholesome device. The teenager needs to understand three things:

• How to recognize manipulation by guilt.

- That this device is unwholesome, unhealthy, and unethical—that it's wrong.

- That the normal and justifiable reaction to manipulation is anger.

In the story about the confrontation between Jesus and the money changers in the temple, I see manipulation as one element that caused Jesus' anger. The people coming to the temple needed to sacrifice to fulfill their religious obligation. They would feel guilty if they didn't offer an animal sacrifice. Merchants who sold animals set up business right in the temple. In the scene Jesus described as a cave full of robbers, there was manipulation by guilt. And Jesus' anger was an appropriate reaction. (See Matt. 21; Mark 11; Luke 19; John 2.)

I remember counseling a beautiful 16-year-old girl named Claudia. She was an extremely sensitive girl and in deep depression. During our conversation, I discovered that her boyfriend used guilt to manipulate her in many ways. As is so typical among teenagers, Claudia was not fully aware of her sensitivity, depression, or of being manipulated by guilt. First I explained to her how sensitive she was—how easy it was to hurt her and to make her feel guilty. Then I explained how others, especially her boyfriend, were able to control her by making her feel guilty if she didn't do what they wanted.

Because Claudia didn't understand at first what I was trying to tell her, I gave her an example that wasn't so close to home. I said, "Claudia, I'm a sensitive person, too, and I didn't learn how some people were able to manipulate me by guilt until a few years ago. After I finished medical school, I wanted to sell my house. I was having difficulty selling it myself, so I contracted a realtor to sell it for me. A few days later, a fellow medical student in my class who was going to remain in that city for an internship offered me a certain price for the home but wanted to bypass the realtor and save the fees. I told him I couldn't do that and that he would have to go through the realtor. Later that day, the realtor came with an offer from another client and I took it. When my classmate found out that I had sold the house, he was furious and tried to talk me into changing my mind and selling it to him. The arguments that he used consisted of reminding me that we were fellow classmates, that I would make more money where I would be interning than he would make, and that the house had five years wear on it and was not worth the price the other person was offering."

Then I said, "Do you see, Claudia, how this man was trying to manipulate me into selling my house to him by making me feel guilty?"

Claudia's eyes lit up. She understood why she had so little control over her own life. The next time I saw Claudia, her depression had lifted and there was a sparkle in her eye. She was learning how to think for herself and to determine her behavior rather than being manipulated by guilt.

Parents must be careful not to manipulate their teenagers by guilt. It's so easy for parents to fall into this trap, especially if they happen to have an extremely sensitive child. A teenager who has been manipulated with guilt by his or her own parents will be easily manipulated by others.

What is the best way to prevent teenagers from being manipulated by guilt? Within the context of unconditional love and focused attention, parents can train their teenagers to identify manipulative behavior in others and to stay free of its trap.

5

Eye Contact and Physical Contact

We live at a time in history of unprecedented numbers of outside influences upon teenagers, many of them unwholesome, and some evil and destructive. A teenager who does not feel loved and cared for is highly vulnerable to these influences. Many unscrupulous users of young people have seduced love-starved teenagers by giving them time, attention, and affection.

The hour is late. As a parent, you have limited time and opportunities to make your teenager feel unconditionally loved. You must be consistent every day in keeping your teenager's emotional tank full. This will enable him or her to grow into a person who can think competently and clearly and develop good self-control. Only when your teenager truly feels that you unconditionally love him or her will you have the influence that you should. Yes, tell your teen, but also *show* your love.

Try to incorporate eye contact and physical contact into all of your everyday dealings with your children. This should be natural, comfortable, and not overdone. Teenagers growing up in a home where parents use eye and physical contact will be comfortable with themselves and other people. They will have an easier time communicating with others and consequently will be well-liked and have high self-esteem.

Appropriate and frequent eye and physical contact are two of the most precious gifts you can give your teenager. Along with focused attention, they are the most effective ways to fill your teenager's emotional tank.

Eye Contact

One of the primary reasons loving parents fail to convey unconditional love is lack of eye contact. Loving, consistent eye contact with your teenager is crucial not only in making good communicational contact, but also in filling emotional needs. Without realizing it, you use eye contact to express many feelings—sadness, anger, hate, rage, and love. In some homes, there is amazingly little eye contact between parents and teenagers. What exists is usually negative, such as when the teenager is being reprimanded or given specific instructions. The more you are able to make eye contact with your teenager as a means of expressing love, the more you will emotionally nourish your teenager with love.

Teenagers vary in their ability to make eye contact. One moment, a teen will eagerly seek it. The next moment, the same teenager may actually avoid your gaze. Within this unevenness, teens are learning patterns of eye contact, primarily from what they observe in their homes from other members of the family.

Some time ago, I saw 17-year-old Bruce. Tall, well built, and good-looking, he was an excellent student and athlete and had a pleasant personality. Strangely enough, with all these things going for him, he had poor self-esteem and considered himself inadequate. It was easy to detect his low opinion of himself simply by observing his pattern of eye contact. His gaze was almost always downward. When he did make eye contact, it was for a fraction of a second. I explained to Bruce that the way he used eye contact strongly affected the way he related to other people. His poor pattern of eye contact actually worsened his self-concept. People felt uncomfortable with Bruce—because of his eye contact pattern, they thought he didn't like them or was ignoring them. They were actually relieved to end a conversation and get away from him. Bruce naturally misinterpreted this as rejection and felt worse than ever. With a steady diet of this pattern over many years, it's no wonder Bruce developed a horrible misrepresentation of himself. Fortunately, it was simple to help Bruce correct his pattern of eye contact.

If teenagers have developed abnormal patterns of eye contact, parents can teach them how they are misapplying them and how to correct them. Good eye contact can make the difference between success and failure in almost all of life's situations.

Giving loving eye contact to your teenager can be difficult, especially during those unpleasant times when he or she is noncommunicative. At times, teenagers can be very difficult to talk with; they merely answer your questions with "uh-huh," "huh-uh," and similar grunts.

These unpleasant times of communication usually grow out of one of three causes:

• The first is regression in psychosexual age. We'll discuss this in chapter 6. The teenager is resolving conflicts that have occurred in the past.

• The second is when the drive for independence is especially strong and the teenager feels a need to separate from parents.

• The third is when the teenager has had an unpleasant experience with peers and feels hurt.

Most likely, along with sullenness, withdrawal, and quietness you'll also see that the teenager is resistant to love and affection from parents.

During these times, it's a mistake to force yourself on your teenager or prod your child with questions. Often a parent will become irritated, worried, and even desperate and try to open up conversation with persistent questions such as: "How did your day go?"; "What happened to you today?"; "Did you have a good time?"; or "Who was there?" This is irritating to anyone who is not in the mood to talk.

The secret is to be available. This means that instead of forcing interaction with your adolescents, be available at all times, so that they can communicate with you when they are comfortable in doing so.

As children enter adolescence, they come under increasing pressure from their drives for independence, sexual expression, and peer acceptance. They must develop defenses against these pressures to keep from being overwhelmed. Unfortunately, they occasionally use rather primitive and unpleasant defenses, such as retreating into states of withdrawal, noncommunication, and sullenness. You can't penetrate or force these primitive defenses without damaging your relationship with the child. The only sensitive, sensible, and constructive way to manage these situations is to wait for the defenses to come down. You must remain available for your teenager to come to you when he or she is able.

You can do definite things to facilitate lowering these defenses, and we will discuss those later. Right now it's important to understand that attempting to batter down this extremely strong defense system is inadvisable.

A teenager's ability to use eye contact varies according to how strong this defense system is. When children are young, they are receptive to eye contact almost continuously. But as they enter into adolescence, there are uneasy periods when they are resistant to eye contact.

Don't let teenagers' occasional tendency to avoid eye contact irritate you. Try simply to accept it, realizing if you remain available, they will come to you when their emotional tanks are dry. At this time, they will be receptive to eye contact and will be communicative. It's important for their self-concept and psychological development for them to know that you will be available when they need you.

Physical Contact

As children become adolescents, they need continual reassurance from their parents that they are loved and accepted. The dilemma for many loving parents is their confusion as to how to meet this need.

Some parents fall into the trap of being overindulgent, providing their teens with things to keep up with their peers, such as a car, stereo, or sporting equipment. These material things may be all right in themselves, but they are no substitute for what teenagers need most—unconditional love. Some parents use overindulgence by permitting, and many times even encouraging, teenagers to go to places and do things that are not healthy for them. For example, I've known many parents who permit, and even encourage, their teens to go to parties designed to arouse sexual desires and where alcoholic beverages and other drugs are served. Few adolescents can handle temptations in these situations, but this type of pressure on our youth is growing. Yet few parents are helping their teenagers. Why? Because they have failed to make their teens feel that they are loved, accepted, and cared for.

Appropriate and consistent physical contact is a vital way to give teenagers that feeling and conviction that you truly care about them. This is especially true when your teenager is noncommunicative, sullen, moody, or resistant. During these times, eye contact may be difficult or even impossible. But physical contact can almost always be used effectively. Seldom does an adolescent respond negatively to a light, brief touch on the shoulder, back, or arm. For example, suppose your son is just sitting in a chair watching TV. What a simple thing to briefly touch him on the shoulder as you walk by. Usually he will not show that he notices it, but it registers in his mind. You can use this vital information to give constant, consistent love by frequent, brief doses of physical contact. You can also use it by occasionally giving longer, more intense nurturing with more prolonged doses of physical contact.

Even when your teenager is in a noncommunicative mood, physical contact can be a means of conveying love. As long as your teenager's focus of attention is directed elsewhere, you are able to give prolonged physical contact regardless of the teenager's mood of receptiveness. For example, suppose your daughter is in an especially difficult state of mind that concerns you. You find an opportunity to talk with her about something that enables you to direct her attention from herself to an object of interest, such as pictures or photographs. You can really take advantage of such situations by putting your hand on her arm, shoulder, or back. You should know your teenager well enough to know how much physical contact he or she can accept at a particular time.

Sometimes your teenager will accept physical contact, but other times may not be able to consciously tolerate your touch. At these times of non-acceptance, you can give physical contact when attention is directed elsewhere so that your teen is unaware of the touch. Even when your teenager is not consciously aware of your physical contact, it registers. Its effect is to help him or her feel, "My mother and father love me and care for me, even during these times when relating to them is hard for me."

There are other ways to provide physical contact with a teenager. Frequently, our 13-year-old David would strain or pull a muscle in a sport. He didn't hesitate to ask me to massage the muscle for him. I was grateful to do so because this gave me a wonderful opportunity to use physical contact. Once, our daughter Carey landed the wrong way on a trampoline and her neck muscles needed rubbing. This was another good opportunity for physical contact.

Fortunately, all our children liked to have their backs scratched. It was genuinely fun to scratch their backs. This has an amazing effect on teens' psychological defenses and also helps tremendously in keeping their emotional tanks full. One summer when David came home from summer camp, what was the first thing he asked for? To have his back scratched and to have his mother and me talk with him and read to him.

Although some parents are unwilling to provide emotional nurture to their teenagers, especially with physical contact, I am very thankful that most parents love their teens enough to provide this for them. It's so simple to do, yet so wonderfully effective.

In certain situations, it's good to hug and kiss your teenager. Although you don't want to do it so often that you make your child uncomfortable, there are times when it's appropriate: when departing or returning from a trip, or when the teenager does something that he or she is especially proud of, such as winning an award. Or when your teenager comes to you feeling deeply hurt, remorseful, or otherwise troubled and seems to need affirming. And, of course, there are times when, for no discernible reason, your teenager simple feels a need for affection. If you are alert to provide it, what a special moment you will have with your child. But you must remain alert for such opportunities because it's sometimes difficult to know when your teenager wants or needs affection.

Many times, your teenager will be subtle in hinting that he or she wants your attention or affection. Your teen may approach you and talk about very superficial or meaningless topics. Usually, this is the key. At that moment, he or she seems so intense, serious, and persistent in mood, and very much out of context, considering the topic of conversation. Be patient. Your teenager is buying time in your presence until psychological defenses have time to come down enough to talk about important and meaningful things. Be careful not to be in a hurry and cut off the communication. Your teenager would naturally interpret this as rejection and your relationship might be harmed. If you are patient and give your teenager the time he or she needs, the superficial conversation will eventually give way to what your child really wants to talk about. You must be an active listener, and this requires patience.

At family conferences, one of the most common questions parents ask me is this: "If I have given my teenager too little eye contact and physical contact, how can I make up for it?" This is a very good question. These parents should not overwhelm their teenagers by suddenly giving large amounts of eye and physical contact. First, they need to obtain a baseline—a general idea of how much eye and physical contact an individual teenager can accept. Starting from there, they will gradually increase contact over the coming weeks and months. The less noticeable the increases are, the better, and the more comfortable the teenager will be.

Someone has said, "Thank goodness adolescence is a time-limited disease." We parents need to hang in there during this period of difficult and intense change. The more we maintain our cool and self-control, the smoother and less traumatic the time will be. Our children will emerge from the teenage years more mature, and our relationships with them will be better when they reach adulthood.

When we remain available to give our teenagers the love they need whenever they can accept it, we demonstrate the manner in which God relates to us. He is constantly available to nurture and help us if we are truly members of his family, even when we are rejecting of him. "If we are unfaithful to Him, He Himself will remain faithful" (2 Tim. 2:13, MLB).

6

Parental Self-Control

Mr. and Mrs. Oliver looked at each other and shook their heads in puzzlement. Not ten minutes before, their 16-year-old daughter, Amy, was explaining precisely how she managed to land a much sought after position by impressing the employer with how mature she was. Now she was crying uncontrollably because her brother had used her shampoo.

Parents of teenagers know that adolescence is a tumultuous time in which the teenager can swing from toddler to adult, from sweet to sour, from logical to irrational, and back again, all within the span of a day—or an hour. These changes can be intense and frequent, and too few parents know exactly why they happen.

In the teenage years, young people are attempting to resolve all conflicts they have previously experienced in their lives, especially with their parents. Although teenagers are not conscious of this desire to resolve old conflicts, the drive within them to do so is so strong that it appears to others that the teenagers have chosen a deliberate course of action.

An early adolescent between the ages of 12 and 15 often will display frequent and unexpected mood shifts. One minute the teen will seem to be very mature, and the next minute like a small child.

Before they can comfortably and normally grow away from their parents and become responsibly independent, teenagers must clear their past, so to speak, of problems and conflicts they have had with people, and especially with their parents.

When our Carey was 13, I noticed one day that her attitude toward me was one of irritability and some hostility. I asked her, "Please tell me, Honey, have I done anything that has upset or hurt you?" Without hesitation, she recounted an incident that occurred six years previously! We were riding in a station wagon; my wife and I were in the front seat, the other children in the middle seat, and Carey with a friend in the back seat. All of the kids were throwing popcorn at each other. Because it was distracting me as I was driving, I yelled for them to stop. Carey exclaimed that I had embarrassed her by "screaming at her friends." Yes, I remembered the incident but never guessed that it had affected her so deeply.

At that moment, Carey had psychologically regressed to a seven-year-old in order to deal with that particular conflict. After she revealed this encounter to me (and I noted the anger in her voice), I told her that I honestly had not realized the embarrassment and pain I had caused her. When I told her I was sorry and asked her forgiveness, she was immediately relieved and became her 13-year-old self again.

This regression and advance in psychological age is one reason why early teenagers are so unpredictable and sometimes difficult to understand. Parents should react to them according to the age they are exhibiting at that time. For instance, let's say your early adolescent son approaches you with a highly sophisticated statement such as, "Dad, what do you think of the Middle East crisis? I wonder if the displaced Palestinian Arab families should be entitled to return to their homes and be a normal part of the Israeli nation." After a couple of gulps, you are able to communicate with him on that exact level and discuss the issue.

But that same teenager may be back 30 minutes later with what appears to be a two-year-old temper tantrum. What do you do? Right! Relate to him as would be appropriate with a two-year-old having a temper tantrum. As you can easily see, this takes real flexibility on your part to change your level of communication rapidly. This is why a good, flexible youth counselor who is dealing with several early adolescents can be utterly exhausted at the end of the day.

It's extremely important that you as a parent exhibit emotional self-control. Emotional overreaction will hurt your relationship with your teenager in several ways:

- Excessive and uncontrolled anger will make it difficult for teenagers to come to you when their emotional tanks need refilling.

- Emotional overreaction tends to cause your adolescent to respect you less—a very natural response to anyone who lacks self-control.

- Losing your cool tends to push your teen into the influence of others, especially peers.

Maintaining Self-Control

But how do you keep yourself in good condition emotionally? How do you maintain self-control? The most common problems that adversely affect an adult's ability to control anger are depression, fatigue, and anxiety. Most people are ineffective in preventing depression because they don't realize how closely it is related to how much time they spend with people and how much time they spend alone. In other words, time balance. Each person has a different need in this regard. Some require more time socially relating to people, while some require more time alone. Unfortunately, I can't think of one person I've come across who was actually aware of this crucial fact. Most people follow this pattern: they find themselves spending more and more time with people, to the point of social saturation. They become more prone to depression because they are emotionally drained and fatigued from the excessive social contact. Depression causes most people to withdraw and become reclusive. This, along with being tired of being around people, causes them to spend too much time alone. But then they feel lonely, yearn to be with people, seek them out, and the cycle starts again. This is one reason few people lead balanced, well-adjusted lives.

Of course, some unfortunate people do not have enough control over their lives to achieve this balance. They may be forced to spend too much time with people because they don't have the means to privacy. Others spend too much time alone because they are old, ill, or don't have access to friends. Either way, depression usually is miserably present.

For the sake of your own mental health and that of your teenager, determine what percentage of your time to spend with people and how much to spend alone. This differs for every person and your own ratio can change with times and seasons and circumstances.

The quality of each kind of time is important also, especially the time alone, which should be emotionally refreshing. This may mean reading a good book, hiking, walking, exercising alone, praying, or meditating. Television seldom fills this need. In fact, TV seems to leave most people even more emotionally drained.

Emotional stability and self-control do not just happen. You must prepare yourself to cope with emotional strain and frustration. A normal teenager will bring forth both. To maintain a healthy relationship with your teenager and keep communication open, you need to be in good control of yourself, especially of your anger. Emotional overreaction is destructive if it happens too often and is not resolved. We all overreact at times, but if we don't do it too often, it's possible to produce a positive situation out of a negative situation. This may involve apologizing to a son or daughter for overreacting and asking for forgiveness: "Honey, I'm sorry I overdid it and yelled yesterday. What you did was wrong, but I overreacted and should have handled it in a calmer way. Will you forgive me?" This approach not only prevents many disasters but can actually strengthen and sweeten a parent-teenager relationship. However, if you overreact too often or in extreme ways, simply saying you're sorry and asking forgiveness won't work; it could even lower your teenager's opinion of you.

The more pleasant you are with your teenager, the firmer you can afford to be in setting limits and in discipline. Likewise, the more unpleasant you are, the less firm you can afford to be. Why? First of all, as we have already stated, the more unpleasant you are, the less your teenager will respect you and the more he or she will be inclined to go against your wishes. Second, the more unpleasant you are, the more parental authority you have dissipated in ventilating your own anger and frustration. In contrast, the more pleasant you are, the more parental authority you have saved to control your teenager's behavior. And this is what you want—good behavioral control! How can you really expect good self-control from your teenager if you don't have it yourself? You'll need energy, preparation, self-discipline, and self-control if you are going to be pleasant in the midst of unpleasant but normal adolescent strivings. Remember those two critical words: *pleasant but firm.* As long as parents are pleasant but firm with teenagers, especially when times are difficult, the fewer problems they'll have with them, and the more teenagers will respect and love parents.

Anger is difficult to control if your spiritual life is not sound. An unhealthy spiritual life can cause depression and anxiety. It can also affect your thought control in such a way that you arrive at wrong decisions or conclusions—including your ideas regarding other people's motives (cynicism). Any of these problems can make you lose spiritual perspective and can hinder your ability to control anger.

A healthy spiritual life is one in which communication is open between you and God. How do you do this? First, make sure you have a clean heart by asking God to search your heart and convict you of any wrong he finds there. Next, confess these wrongs and obtain God's forgiveness and cleansing. This clears the channel of communication between you and God. Now you are ready to draw close to him and he to you. God is then able to fill your emotional and spiritual tank. He does this by being with you, close to you, listening, guiding, comforting, and reassuring you with his promises and love.

It takes time to fellowship with God long enough to really know him and for him to fill you and prepare you for your responsibilities as a parent.

I find it very difficult to spend time alone with God without distractions. When my children were young, my time for emotional and spiritual refreshment with my heavenly Father often happened after all the kids were in bed, usually between 9 and 9:30 at night. To escape distractions, I often take a walk or just sit outside, weather permitting, or in a quiet room. It usually takes 10 to 20 minutes of solitude to feel close to God, to quiet my inner self after a typically hectic day. God doesn't hurry or rush. He is so calm and he continues to speak in a still, small voice.

Your ability to handle anger is influenced by many things, most of which have little or nothing to do with your teenager. One of these is your physical condition. Are you eating foods that will help you feel your best? I've seen many people who believe their diets are healthy, when in actuality they are not. Most authorities consider breakfast the most important meal of the day. What you eat for breakfast strongly influences how you feel the rest of the day. Most people eat too much carbohydrate and not enough protein and bulk for breakfast. This usually produces a lack of energy later and induces them to seek stimulants such as coffee or soft drinks (many soft drinks have caffeine in them). Caffeine has differing effects on people, but none of them aid the emotional stability and calmness you need with your teenager. Therefore, eating a healthy, low carbohydrate breakfast with plenty of protein and bulk and avoiding caffeine are a good start in gaining self-control.

Many people feel that they are doing themselves a favor by skipping breakfast or even lunch. Skipping meals does not aid in weight reduction or promote a sense of well being. For lunch, it's important not to eat too much carbohydrate and to avoid caffeine. An excessive carbohydrate diet will sap energy. Caffeine will increase irritability. It's amazing how much better I feel from lunch to supper on a green salad rather than a sandwich or hamburger.

Supper is the meal at which most people tend to overeat. This is one reason why a healthy breakfast and lunch are important. If your carbohydrate intake has been excessive or you have skipped breakfast or lunch, you may not be able to control your dietary intake later in the day, especially in the midst of depression or fear. And, of course, if you eat improperly at these times, you will not feel your best during the evening.

A regular exercise program, a good diet, recreation, and maintaining a healthy spiritual life can go a long way toward preventing depression and other emotional imbalances. Unfortunately, not all depression can be prevented. Many people are biochemically or hereditarily prone to depression. People who have done all in their power to prevent depression yet become depressed should seek help—not only for their own sake but also for the sake of their families. A moderately to severely depressed parent simply cannot handle a normal teenager well. The relationship between parent and child will suffer, and so will the teenager.

An Angry Father

Bob was a 17-year-old boy I counseled because of drug usage, poor grades, and a defiant attitude. When I saw him alone, he was a calm, polite boy and exceptionally easy to communicate with. I felt he was truthful when he stated that he did not like his behavior and wanted to change. He said that he had been trying to make a change in his behavior. But after bouts of fighting and arguing with his father—which were daily occurrences—he would become so angry that all he could think of was getting back by doing the very things his father (and Bob) did not like. Of course, I wanted to check out Bob's perceptions and see if they were accurate. So I asked Bob's parents to join us.

Bob's father was an extraordinarily angry man. He immediately made a grossly hostile remark about Bob's "terrible and unacceptable behavior." His anger and the ferocity of his remarks continued and even increased. Bob made no response, but deep, painful anger was obviously welling up inside him. Finally, Bob's mother tried to intervene by telling the father that Bob's behavior had been good recently and that she could not understand why he was so angry. Also, I noticed that the behavior about which the father was complaining did not justify such vehement condemnation. The father not only ignored the mother's pleas but also used Bob's behavior as an excuse to rid himself of excessive anger. When I talked with the father alone, I learned the real cause of his frustration. He was having severe problems at work, was extremely depressed, could not sleep well, could hardly eat, tired easily, and felt life was not worth living. Bob was the only "safe" place to vent his misery. I don't know which one made my heart ache most—Bob, his mother, or his father.

It's common for teenagers to be receptacles of parents' displaced anger. Teenagers often tend to put pressure on us, make us tense, upset, and angry. Therefore, sometimes it seems justifiable to dump accumulated anger on them. This is so dangerous! Excessive and overreactive anger is an enemy of parents seeking to relate to their teenagers. Nothing else cuts off parent-adolescent communication the way poorly controlled anger does.

Most parents seem to assume that their teenagers don't need their love and affection as they did as small children. This simply is not true. Teenagers continue to need love, affection, assurance, and care as never before, even though in their biological drive for independence, they may sometimes act as though they don't.

I made that mistake with Carey. Her eighteenth birthday and graduation from high school occurred at about the same time. In my mind, I unconsciously graduated her from being my child to an independent adult. Fortunately, my wife, Pat, noticed the effect of this. I was not as loving or caring with Carey as before; this hurt her because she felt that she had done something wrong. Pat told me about this and, thank goodness, I was able to again relate to her as a daughter—as my child.

We never grow out of the need to be loved and cared for. These needs may be gradually taken over by other people in adult life. But during the years when our children are dependent on us, we parents must always stand available and ready to love and nourish them whenever we're needed, especially during the teenage years.

7

Teenage Anger

Many parents assume that anger in a teenager is bad or abnormal and that they should not allow their children to express it. This is a dangerous error. Scripture instructs us to "train up a child in the way he should go," to educate him "according to his life requirements" (Prov. 22:6, KJV and MLB). One of the most important areas in which a teenager needs training is in how to handle anger.

The feeling of anger is not bad or good in itself. Anger is normal and occurs in every human being. The problem is not the anger itself but how to manage it. This is where most people have problems. It's imperative to understand the different ways to handle anger and know which ways are best.

Passive-Aggressive Behavior

Let's start with what I consider the absolutely worst way to handle anger: passive-aggressive behavior. This is a professional term you should add to your vocabulary. Passive-aggressive behavior is the opposite of an open, honest, direct, and verbal expression of anger. Passive-aggressive behavior is an expression of anger that gets back at a person indirectly. Mild examples of this are procrastination, dawdling, stubbornness, intentional inefficiency, and "forgetfulness."

The subconscious purpose of passive-aggressive behavior on the part of a child or teenager is to upset the parents or parent figures and make them angry. Passive-aggressive behavior is a refusal to take responsibility for one's own behavior. It is the determination to do exactly opposite of what the legitimate authority figure wants.

Passive-aggressive techniques of handling anger are indirect, cunning, self-defeating, and destructive. Unfortunately, passive-aggressive behavior is subconsciously motivated; that is, the child or teenager is not consciously aware of using this resistant, obstructive behavior to release pent-up anger and to upset parents.

Passive-aggressive behavior is at the crux of most problems with today's teenagers, from poor grades to drugs to sexual misconduct to suicide. Of course, there are other causes of adolescent problems, so it is important to be able to clearly identify PA behavior when it occurs. It is usually handled quite differently from other causes of teenage misbehavior.

First of all, consider the fact that passive-aggressive behavior is irrational—it doesn't make logical sense. A good example of this is a student who is really capable of good grades, wants to make good grades, tries to make good grades, but makes poor grades. It makes no logical sense.

Second, you can begin to label it passive-aggressive behavior when nothing works no matter what the authority figure does to correct it. This is because the underlying, subconscious motive is to upset the parent or other authority figure. In the example of the student who should make good grades but doesn't, no matter what the parent and teacher do to help the ailing student, nothing works: rewards, punishment, a change of curriculum, or even a tutor doesn't result in better grades. Since the real motivation is to upset the parent or teacher, subconsciously the student will make sure nothing works, no matter what steps parents take.

It's so important to identify passive-aggressive behavior. For example, passive aggression in the student who could make good grades but doesn't affects the entire future of that teenager. Tragically, if a teenager does not learn to handle anger maturely and grow out of the PA stage by the age of 16 or 17, this trait will harden and become a permanent part of his or her personality. He or she will use PA behavior toward future professors, employers, spouses, children, and so on. This leads to serious problems for the individual to cope with everyday life and results in endless misery for those associated with him or her.

Because few people have been properly trained in handling anger, most of us handle anger with about the same maturity as we did in adolescence and thus we suffer from our own PA traits, of which we are mostly unaware. We could use help in this area ourselves, right? Ask your spouse or best friend.

One of the earliest ways a child can show passive-aggressive tendencies is by soiling his or her pants after being toilet-trained. In many such cases, parents have prohibited the child from expressing any anger, especially verbally. Then, if the parents have overreacted by becoming excessively angry or even punishing the child whenever he or she expresses anger openly, what can the child do with normally occurring anger?

A child in this situation may use passive-aggressive behavior to get back at parents in ways that will upset them, like soiling pants—a very effective but unhealthy way to express anger. There's little the parents can do in such a situation. Because they have refused to permit the child to openly and directly express anger, the child has been forced to use an indirect, harmful way to do it, and the parents have backed themselves into a corner. The more the parents punish the child, the more he or she will soil pants. Why? Because the subconscious purpose of passive-aggressive behavior is to upset the parents. What a dilemma! God pity both the parent and child in such a situation.

Many older children who use passive-aggressive means to express anger do poor work in school. Their attitude is, "You can lead a horse to water, but you can't make him drink. You can make me go to school, but you can't make me get good grades." The children's anger is in control, and the parents are utterly helpless. The more the parents become upset—the subconscious purpose of all this—the worse the situation becomes.

It's important to know that the passive-aggressive child does not do these things consciously or purposefully. They are part of an unconscious process he or she is not aware of and into which he or she has been forced by parents.

Passive-aggressive behavior in younger children is bad enough, but passive-aggressive behavior in teenagers can be utterly disastrous. I've seen this unhealthy way of handling anger cause teenagers to run the gamut—from making poor grades to using drugs, becoming pregnant, committing crimes, and attempting suicide. There are, of course, other causes for these types of behavior. The passive-aggressive tendency, however, is a most serious cause that is on the increase among teenagers.

Many teenagers do poorly in school because their parents have made themselves unapproachable—either by their own emotional overreaction or by being intolerant in not allowing their teenagers to express negative or unpleasant feelings. Teenagers break parental rules, including habitually coming in late, not because of a normal drive for independence, but as a way to upset their parents and express their anger indirectly. I've seen girls who got pregnant as an act of anger toward parents because they were never allowed to express unpleasant feelings, especially anger. I've seen teenagers who developed antisocial and antiauthority attitudes as a means to express anger.

More complexly, I've seen teenagers turn their unresolved anger onto themselves to cause psychosomatic problems such as headaches, ulcers, and skin problems. And most tragically, I've seen this passive-aggressive behavior so ingrained in teenagers that it becomes their primary way of handling any anger-provoking situation that may confront them, even to the point of committing suicide as a means to indirectly express anger.

Some time ago, I saw a 16-year-old girl whose parents mistakenly thought they were raising their daughter correctly by refusing to allow her to express any unpleasant feelings, especially anger. They thought they would teach her to be a happy person by learning to express only pleasant feelings. She learned to avoid open expression of her anger to the source of her frustration; she would habitually express her anger in ways that would indirectly hurt the person who caused her anger. This became such a habit that most of her behavior was understandable only by knowing that she was trying to hurt someone indirectly. What finally brought her to seek help was her sixth suicide attempt. Each of the attempts was planned to make a particular person feel guilty, upset, and hurt. The first five attempts were half-hearted and no great threat to her life. However, the sixth resulted in her being in a coma and near death for several days. As I talked with her after she recovered, I saw that her conduct definitely puzzled her. She did not understand that her behavior was a long-established pattern of expressing anger in unhealthy, self-defeating, destructive, indirect, and displaced ways.

Passive-aggressive behavior is common. Why? Because most people do not understand anger or know what to do with it. They feel that anger is somehow wrong or sinful and should be "disciplined" out of a child. This is a serious misunderstanding because the feeling of anger is normal and has been experienced by everyone since Adam and Eve. If, when your teenager becomes angry and you yell: "Stop that kind of talk. I will not allow it!" what can your teenager do? Only two things—disobey you and continue to "talk that way," or obey you and "stop talking that way." If your teen chooses the latter and ceases to express anger, the anger will not go away. The teen will simply suppress the anger into the subconscious where it will remain unresolved, waiting to be expressed later through inappropriate and/or passive-aggressive behavior.

Another mistake some parents make related to teaching their children about expressing anger is the inappropriate use of humor. Whenever a situation becomes tense, especially if someone is becoming angry, many parents will interject humor to relieve the tension. Of course, humor is a wonderful asset in any family. But where it is consistently used to escape handling anger appropriately, teenagers simply cannot learn how to appropriately deal with it.

I once visited a home where the father of the family had an uncommonly humorous wit. Whenever his wife or one of his teenagers began expressing an unpleasant feeling, he would come up with a hilarious statement. Consequently, none of the teenagers in that family could deal with anger and resorted to passive-aggressive means of expressing it indirectly. Whenever the boy would experience frustration or anger-provoking situations, he would have severe headaches. The girl manifested her anger indirectly by voluntarily helping her mother with housework but doing such a poor job that she often caused the mother more work than if she had not helped at all.

Passive-aggressive behavior easily becomes an ingrained, habitual pattern that can last a lifetime. Teenagers who avoid honestly and openly dealing with anger in an appropriate manner may use passive-aggressive techniques in every relationship. This can affect relationships later with spouses, children, work associates, and friends. What a tragedy! And most of these unfortunate people are not fully aware of their self-defeating patterns of behavior or their problems with handling anger.

Incidentally, one of the most common and dangerous types of passive-aggressiveness is seen in driving habits. Have you ever noticed how some people speed up when you try to pass them? Or how about the driver on the highway who passes you and then darts in front of you, forcing you to use your brakes to avoid running into him? These may be blatant examples of passive-aggressive behavior. Needless to say, it's difficult to appreciate a passive-aggressive person.

This brings to mind a 39-year-old woman named Margaret. She was born and reared in a Christian home. Unfortunately, her parents believed that a child should not be permitted to express anger. So she never learned how to properly handle or resolve it. Consequently, she has developed into an individual whose overall behavior pattern is designed to upset her parents. Her whole life is aimed at doing the exact opposite of what her parents would want. Her behavior patterns are unconscious, or out of her awareness. Consciously, she thinks of herself as a well-meaning Christian who earnestly desires to live a proper lifestyle. However, she has had one affair after another with married men. She has been indicted for embezzlement and fraud. Margaret is an enigma to herself. Until therapy, she could not understand why her lifestyle and behavioral patterns were entirely inconsistent with her basic beliefs. Hers is a wasted life of self-abasement and self-destruction because her primary purpose in living is to behave in ways just the opposite of what her parents would want her to be. And she is not consciously aware of it. Tragic!

Passive-aggressive behavior is absolutely the worst way to express anger for several reasons:

• It can easily become an ingrained, tenacious pattern of behavior that will last a lifetime.

- It can distort a person's personality and make him a quite dis-
agreeable person.

- It can interfere in all the teenager's future relationships.

- It is one of the most difficult behavioral disorders to correct.

Scripture instructs us to train a child in the way he should go. Forcing a child to suppress the anger and not deal with it properly is training him in the way he should *not* go. It's crucial to train a child in the proper way to handle anger. You can do this by teaching your teenager to resolve the anger, not to suppress it.

The Anger Ladder

There are many more ways to express anger than in a passive-aggressive manner. The more immature a person is, the more immaturely he or she will express anger. The more mature the person is, the more maturely he or she will express anger. Handling anger appropriately and maturely is one of the most difficult lessons in becoming a mature person—one that most adults never learn.

Children will tend to express anger immaturely until trained to do otherwise. A teenager cannot be expected to automatically express anger in the best, most mature way. But this is what parents are expecting when they simply tell their teen not to get mad. Parents must train teenagers to take one step at a time in learning to deal with anger.

The Anger Ladder illustrates the different steps or levels of maturity in expressing anger and helps parents see that a teenager must be trained to progress from one rung or level of maturity to the next, as he or she expresses anger more and more appropriately.

1. Passive-aggressive behavior is the worst way to express anger. (In some cases, sociopathy, including deliberate homicide, may be worse; but this is rare in early adolescence, totally abnormal, and beyond the scope of this chapter.)

2. A slightly better way to express anger is to be utterly out of control behaviorally in such a way that the person is in a fit of rage, actually destroys property, or is violent toward another person. As bad as this may sound, passive-aggressive behavior is worse. Why? Because rageous behavior is much easier to deal with, correct, and prevent than passive-aggressive behavior.

3. A somewhat better way to express anger is to be in a fit of rage, but maintain enough self-control to prevent property destruction and personal violence. The outburst is confined to yelling, screaming, or cursing in such a way as to verbally hurt someone, perhaps with name-calling or accusatory remarks. The anger is expressed not only at the person with whom we are angry but at anyone who happens to be in the vicinity. As poor and immature as these methods are in expressing anger, they are far better than passive-aggressive behavior or other ways of displaying anger behaviorally.

4. The next better way to handle anger is uncontrollably ventilating it verbally but without seeking to hurt anyone verbally, as with name-calling or criticizing. In this situation, the anger is directed not only toward the source of the anger but toward anyone who happens to be around. As primitive and poor as this method is, it is better than any yet mentioned.

5. A somewhat better way to handle anger is to ventilate it unpleasantly, perhaps by yelling and screaming, but confining the remarks to the provoking issue, and, if possible, toward the person provoking the anger. Of course, whether expressing the anger toward the person who has angered the teenager is appropriate or not depends on the particular situation.

6. The best way to express anger is to do it verbally, as pleasantly and rationally as possible, and toward the person one is angry at. You hope that the person receiving the anger will respond in an equally mature way, attempt to understand the other's position, and that the two can resolve the issue. Resolving the issue means for both parties to rationally and logically examine the issue, discuss it, understand it from both points of view, and to come to an agreement on what to do about it. This takes a great deal of maturity on both sides. Few people ever come to this point of maturity in their lives.

I have found that describing the different levels of maturity in expressing anger becomes very complex and difficult to understand. To simplify it as much as possible and yet give you a workable knowledge of it, I have created an Anger Ladder.

The list of 15 ways of behaving while angry are combined in various arrangements on the Anger Ladder. Notice that most expressions of anger are primarily negative. On the ladder, only the top two rungs are totally positive.

1. Pleasant behavior
2. Seeking resolution
3. Focusing anger on source only
4. Holding to the primary complaint
5. Thinking logically and constructively
6. Unpleasant and loud behavior
7. Cursing
8. Displacing anger to sources other than the original
9. Expressing unrelated complaints
10. Throwing objects
11. Destroying property
12. Verbal abuse
13. Emotionally destructive behavior
14. Physical abuse
15. Passive-aggressive behavior

Each rung on the Anger Ladder represents a progressively better way to express anger. You want to train your teenager to take one step at a time, to go up one rung at a time. How do you do this?

As parents, you should be good examples in the proper expression of anger. Also, you can expect your teenager to become angry at times. Instead of forbidding your teen to become angry or overreacting to anger, meet your child where he or she is the ability to handle anger

POSITIVE

1. PLEASANT • SEEKING RESOLUTION • FOCUSING ANGER ON SOURCE • HOLDING TO PRIMARY COMPLAINT • THINKING LOGICALLY

2. PLEASANT • FOCUSING ANGER ON SOURCE • HOLDING TO PRIMARY COMPLAINT • THINKING LOGICALLY

POSITIVE AND NEGATIVE

3. FOCUSING ANGER ON SOURCE • HOLDING TO PRIMARY COMPLAINT • THINKING LOGICALLY • unpleasant, loud

4. HOLDING TO PRIMARY COMPLAINT • THINKING LOGICALLY • unpleasant, loud • displacing anger to other sources

5. FOCUSING ANGER ON SOURCE • HOLDING TO PRIMARY COMPLAINT • THINKING LOGICALLY • unpleasant, loud • verbal abuse

6. THINKING LOGICALLY • unpleasant, loud • displacing anger to other sources • expressing unrelated complaints

PRIMARILY NEGATIVE

7. unpleasant, loud • displacing anger to other sources • expressing unrelated complaints • emotionally destructive behavior

8. unpleasant, loud • displacing anger to other sources • expressing unrelated complaints • verbal abuse • emotionally destructive behavior

9. unpleasant, loud • cursing • displacing anger to other sources • expressing unrelated complaints • verbal abuse • emotionally destructive behavior

10. FOCUSING ANGER ON SOURCE • unpleasant, loud • cursing • displacing anger to other sources • throwing objects • emotionally destructive behavior

11. unpleasant, loud • cursing • displacing anger to other sources • throwing objects • emotionally destructive behavior

NEGATIVE

12. FOCUSING ANGER ON SOURCE • unpleasant, loud • cursing • destroying property • verbal abuse • emotionally destructive behavior

13. unpleasant, loud • cursing • displacing anger to other sources • destroying property • verbal abuse • emotionally destructive behavior

14. unpleasant, loud • cursing • displacing anger to other sources • destroying property • verbal abuse • physical abuse • emotionally destructive behavior

15. passive-aggressive behavior

and train your child from there. For example:

One teenager handles anger at the level of Rung 6 on the Anger Ladder. That is, this teenager is unpleasant about it, expresses it at inappropriate people (for example, at a little brother instead of at the person who angered him), sticks to the primary complaint only (that is, only what is bothering him or her), and is logical and constructive (trying to make things better, not worse).

You then determine what improvement you want for your teenager. In this example, you want the teen to learn to direct anger toward the appropriate person and not take it out on a younger brother.

To train the teen in this situation, find a time soon after you both have calmed down and the atmosphere is pleasant. At this best of possible moments, compliment and praise your teenager in the areas of expressing anger that he or she did correctly. Then ask your teenager to correct that one selected aspect you want changed—in this case, taking anger out on a younger brother.

We all must develop our own ways of training teenagers in handling anger maturely. Consider ways I eventually found worked best for me. When one of my teenagers verbalized his or her anger and I saw something that needed correcting, I would, as soon as possible, find a time when we were both calm and relaxed. First, I let my teenager know that bringing the anger to me verbally was fine, so the teen wouldn't feel he or she had done something wrong and be reluctant to verbalize anger again. I would say something like, "I'm glad you brought your anger to me. When you are happy, your mother and I want to know you're happy. When you're sad, we want to know that. And when you are angry, we want to know you're angry."

Second, I sought to reinforce appropriate ways my teenagers expressed anger and praise them for it. Remember, when a teenager is expressing anger verbally, there are a lot of things he or she is doing right. I would then say something like this: "I'm proud of the way you handled your anger. You didn't take it out on your little brother or the dog or throw anything or bring up unrelated facts. You clearly told me what was on your mind regarding this problem. That's good."

Now I was ready to help my teenager take the next step up the anger ladder. Please remember, this is a five- or six-year project, and a teen can take only one step at a time. So I would determine what step I would like him or her to take next, and I would *ask* the teenager, not tell. For example, I would say something like, "The only thing you did wrong, Son, was to call me that name. When you're angry, please just call me 'Dad.'" This is critical. I couldn't automatically expect that the very next time my teenager verbalized anger, he or she would have made that step. It may have taken several incidents. Remember, maturation is slow, gradual, difficult, and often painful. But eventually your teenager will emerge (hopefully at 16 or 17) a responsible, cooperative, mature person. "No pain, no gain."

This reminds me of a saying by Mark Twain, if I may paraphrase it: "When I was fifteen years old, my father was the most ignorant person I knew. But it was amazing how much he learned in the next five years." Folks, that is adolescence!

Let me clarify one point of possible confusion. It is in verbal expression of anger that you need to train your teenager so that he or she learns to handle it better. I am not encouraging permissiveness in behavior. You must remain firm in not allowing your teenager to behave inappropriately. Limit setting regarding behavior must be firm and consistent. This distinction between verbal and behavioral expressions of anger is critical.

David

Like most people, I have my moments when anger is a problem for me—anger within me and anger in others. However, here is one experience I believe I handled correctly. And, best of all, I gained tremendous insight into the whole area of a child's anger. Our son David was overloaded with homework one day when he was 13. He arrived home at about 3:30 that afternoon, and except for ten minutes for supper, was still working on academics at 11:30 that night. He also had a book report due in a few days. At 11:30, I said, "David, I don't care how much homework you still have to do, you need your sleep and I want you in bed now."

He replied, "Please give me five more minutes, Dad; I'm almost finished."

I said, "OK, five more minutes and that's it."

I then returned to my bedroom with my wife. In a few minutes, David came into the room with a book in his hand, walked up to his mother, and said, "Mom, I think I'll use this book for my book report."

His mother looked at the book and replied, "No, David, you can't use that book because it's the same one you used last year."

David said, "I know, but I can make another book report on it and won't have to read a new book."

"I'm sorry, David," his mother replied, "that wouldn't be right. You have to read another book."

David became angry and answered his mother rudely. "OK, I'll read it. Just help me find another book and I'll read it. OK, I'll read another book!"

My first reaction was a typical one toward a child who was verbally ventilating anger in an unpleasant, loud way—I felt the anger rise within me. My first thought was, How dare he talk to his mother that way! I'll show him that he can't get away with being nasty like that.

But fortunately, I remembered a previous event. Three days earlier, I became so infuriated at a man (and at church, mind you!) that I called him a liar. Who handled his anger better? David or I? Then I realized that David had managed his anger better than I had and that he was on Rung 3 on the Anger Ladder. I was near Rung 5. He directed his anger at its source—his mother. He didn't take it out on his little brother, kick his dog, destroy property, attempt to hurt his mother with names or criticism, or use passive-aggressive behavior. He didn't bring up unpleasant subjects or previous grievances. He simply stated that he would read another book. Who can improve on that? The only thing David did wrong was to speak loudly to his mother. Not many people, mature adults included, can beat that.

Now what would have happened if I had lit into David and punished him? I'll tell you. Because he was on Rung 3 of the Anger Ladder, the next time he got angry, he would have been forced to use a more immature way of expressing his anger at a lower level on the Anger Ladder.

Then what should I do? The best thing for me to do at that time was to not respond. Not responding does not mean condoning. By the look on my face and on his mother's face, he knew we didn't like what he was doing. By not responding we were telling David, "We don't like what you are doing, but if you choose to do so, go ahead. It is not bad enough to stop, but we don't like it."

After we all calmed down, David went to bed. During our usual nighttime ritual (here's a good example where nighttime rituals pay off) and after we had prayed together, I said to David, "I was very proud of the way you handled your anger tonight. You didn't take it out on your brother or the dog. You didn't throw anything or sulk, or say anything wrong. You spoke directly to your mother without trying to hurt her with names or criticism. You simply said you would read another book. That's great. The only thing you did wrong was to yell at your mother." The effect was great. David felt relieved that I wasn't angry with him but also felt very bad about yelling at his mother. The next day he apologized to her.

Train Your Teenager

When your teenager expresses anger directly by verbal means, be glad. The more he uses verbalizations to express his anger, the better it is. Then determine where your teen is functioning on the Anger Ladder. Determine in what ways he is expressing anger appropriately and in what ways he is being inappropriate.

It is easy to confuse the verbal expression of anger with disrespect, a stumbling block for most parents. To cope with this dilemma, ask yourself, "What is my teenager's attitude toward me the majority of the time? Is it respectful or disrespectful?" In the vast majority of our teenagers, the answer is respectful. Most teenagers have a basic, respectful attitude toward their parents. If this is the case with your teenager, please relax on this issue and realize that when he or she verbalizes anger—especially anger about a particular item—this is what you want. Then you will be able to train your teenager to mature in this area and to be able to handle anger maturely. On the other hand, if your teenager has a disrespectful attitude toward you most of the time, this is a different issue altogether. This means there is a serious problem in your relationship, and I advise you to get professional help as soon as possible.

Another way to consider this is to look at the teenager who, for some reason, is unable to express anger verbally. This makes it difficult and sometimes impossible to train this teen in becoming mature in handling anger. In fact, one of the first challenges is enabling this type of teenager to express anger verbally. This is extremely difficult. So do you see why we should be glad when a teenager has the ability to express anger verbally? Because then we can train him or her to maturity.

You want to train your teens in the way they should go. First, praise them for appropriate ways they express anger. Then you can talk about one of the inappropriate ways they are using anger (such as name-calling) and ask them to correct it. You want to choose the best possible moment; then talk with your teenager about correcting one item at a time. You are training your child to gradually go up the Anger Ladder one rung at a time.

A certain amount of passive-aggressive behavior is normal in early adolescence—as long as this behavior does not bring harm to anyone, including the teenager or family members. Normal adolescent PA behavior usually starts gradually around the age of 11. Remember that we want the teen to be out of this PA stage around 16 or 17. Therefore, it becomes obvious that this is not a short-term project. We're talking in the range of at least five or six years. This is important to realize because we must be patient and expect slow, gradual improvement—about three steps forward, two steps back progress. This is because learning to handle anger is a maturational process, and we all mature very slowly. So please, don't be impatient with your teenager's progress or you will become quite frustrated and unwittingly destroy the whole process. Be patient!

Most parents expect their children to handle anger maturely, at the highest rung, with no training. This is like saying to a tennis student before his first lesson, "I believe you should be about ready for Wimbledon by now."

In some cases, it's impossible to resolve anger, as for example, when the person provoking the anger is inaccessible. At these times, the teenager must learn other appropriate ways to vent the anger, such as exercise, talking it over with a mature person, using diversion such as an enjoyable activity, or spending time alone in a relaxed manner.

Another way to train a teenager in handling anger is to teach the art of preventing certain types of anger cognitively. This means using active intellectual reasoning to reduce the anger. For example, I saw a wonderful change in David's ability to control anger in his early teens. Instead of strictly reacting emotionally, he learned to use his thought processes more.

In his early teens, David would occasionally lose his temper when playing baseball if another player did something that was obviously wrong, especially if it resulted in physical pain to David. But one summer evening I noticed a degree of progress. In a Little League game, David was running to home plate when the catcher caught the throw from the outfield. He was ready to tag David out when David suddenly surprised the catcher by jumping over his glove. Unfortunately in doing this, he also jumped over home plate. He was on his stomach reaching back to touch the plate when the catcher, infuriated at being tricked, hit David in the face while tagging him. I was stunned and was afraid that David, being the larger boy, would overreact with violence. Much to my relief and amazement, he just dusted himself off and calmly walked to the dugout. David had learned to intellectually nip the anger in the bud by realizing that this particular player had difficulty handling anger and would express it inappropriately. In short, David knew that the catcher did not have anything against him personally and had acted this way because of his own problems with behavior.

Most adults handle their strong anger in inappropriate ways. They may lose control of themselves and vent their anger toward the wrong person. They may hurt the people at whom they are angry behind their backs by using passive-aggressive behavior in some indirect and immature way. Why? Because no one trained them in the better ways to handle anger. Who failed to train them? Their parents.

However, at this point we must be aware that some children are more naturally prone to have difficulties handling anger than others—regardless of the type of parenting they've had. For example, young children and teenagers with certain neurological problems are especially prone to handling anger in passive-aggressive ways. This is especially true, and quite frequent, if there is a history of perceptual or learning problems. These children and teenagers (and later adults) tend to have problems with passive-aggressive behavior and depression.

You see immature ways of handling anger every day. You see a wife and husband yelling, screaming, and cursing at each other. You see the wife or husband having an affair to get back at the other. You see an employee doing poor work to undermine the employer's interests. You see a principal abusing a teacher. You see a teacher subtly working against a principal. You see special interest groups attempting to materially hurt others. Immature handling of anger is on every hand. It is one of the greatest problems in business today, resulting in poor attitudes in employer and employee alike. Sixty to eighty percent of problems in any organization are personnel related because so few people learned how to deal with anger maturely. Most are very good at hiding it superficially when dealing face to face with others; but out it comes later in inappropriate ways.

One of the most important things to understand about anger, whether we are dealing with employees, unions, government agencies, or teenagers, is that it's bound to occur. It can result from any human interaction. The next important fact is that it will tend to build up and become more and more difficult to control, even explosive, if not dealt with. And the more difficult it is to control, the more destructive it may become. Therefore, we must find ways to either "nip it in the bud" if the anger is based on misunderstanding, or to see that the anger is ventilated slowly and then resolved if it is justified. Such control does not come naturally to anyone. We have to learn the maturity that comes with managing anger appropriately through much time and practice.

8

From Parent Control to Self-Control

As a child moves into the teenage years, we hope that discipline and training will gradually change from a parent-control basis to a parent-trust basis in which privileges and freedom depend on trustworthiness. When a child is young and has little judgment to exercise in actions, the parents take almost all the responsibility in determining behavior. As the child becomes a preadolescent and experiences the drive toward independence, he or she will attempt to exert more and more control and decision-making regarding actions. Parents should work to make this transition as smooth and nontraumatic as possible.

To accomplish this, you must first accept the fact that this drive for independence is normal. Eventually, your child should become quite independent of you, whether you like it or not. What you want to be able to do is to control the rate of this gain of independence, gauging it on your teen's rate of maturity. The best indicator you have in doing this is the degree to which you can trust your youngster's ability to control his or her behavior.

Your teen will likely test your limits of control as well as your love for him or her. So, naturally, your great concern is where to set the limits. Should you make them fair, broad, and reasonable? Or should you be very strict? It's important to remember that a normal teenager will test—and sometimes even break—limits or rules, regardless of where you place them. If you make the rules extremely restrictive, your teenager will surely test them, and usually break them. If you make them broad, your teenager will again find some way to challenge them or break them. Common sense, then, indicates that since it is in the makeup of most teenagers to challenge or break rules, no matter how strict or broad they are, the sensible thing is to make rules initially quite strict and restrictive. Then, as the maturing child demonstrates that he or she can be trusted to behave appropriately, you can gradually allow increased privileges with less and less parental control. In other words, privileges will be contingent upon showing you that he or she is trustworthy. As your teenager proves to be more trustworthy, you trust more. As your teenager demonstrates appropriate behavior, you increase privileges. But in order to do this, you must begin from a restrictive position.

There are many advantages to using this approach. First, it's wise to be in the position of being able to allow more privileges and not fewer. Your relationship with your teenager is better when you are able to be positive; it is less comfortable when you must be negative. When your teen is just beginning the adolescent career, especially a social life, if you begin by being somewhat over-restrictive, then you can afford to be positive and grant privileges—you can be the "good guy." However, if you begin by being "broadminded, reasonable, understanding," allowing your budding teenager too many privileges and too few restrictions, you have only one way to go—toward increased restrictiveness or being the "bad guy." Also, if your limits are too broad and lenient, and your teenager breaks them, he or she will be much more likely to bring harm or disgrace on self and family.

I can't overemphasize how important it is to set up the rules that allow you to be as positive as possible. Begin in an over-restrictive way so that you may be able to grant more and more privileges. If you give all the privileges initially, you have nothing to work with. You have no way to reward your teen for taking increased responsibility. And, worse, you have no means to train your child to be trustworthy and learn the value of being responsible.

Your goal in moving from restrictiveness to privilege is that your teenager will act as a responsible, trustworthy, independent adult by the age of 18.

This is not easy, for it takes courage and determination to make your teenager's privileges strictly dependent upon ability to control his or her own behavior. It takes strength for you to stand against the pressure for unearned concessions, not only from your teenager, but from other teenagers, other parents, and even society.

But mark this: all teenagers at some level of consciousness realize they need guidance and control from their parents. They want it. I have heard numerous teenagers say that their parents do not love them because they are not strict or firm enough. And so many teenagers express their thankfulness and love to parents who showed their care and concern by their guidance and control.

Experiencing Consequences

Another factor to consider is that in order for your teenager to continue to develop a normal conscience and learn to behave responsibly as an adult, he or she must experience consequences for behavior—positive consequences for appropriate, responsible behavior; and negative consequences for inappropriate, irresponsible behavior. These consequences must be consistent and fair, and based on behavior, not on how you are feeling at the time. Again, we're back to facing the importance of parental self-control and making decisions based on clear, logical thinking rather than on our impulsive feelings.

How do you accomplish this?

I believe that a rule or decision deserves a reason. A teenager is entitled to know why. And parents must be careful to be sure that the reason is practical and not simply moralistic. Of course, there may be moralistic reasons behind the rule, but there must also be a practical reason. Teenagers in early adolescence are in the midst of questioning their parents' rules and values. And these early teens relate much better to practical rules than to moralistic ones. One reason so many teenagers turn against spiritual values is that they are given too many moralistic reasons for rules and restrictions. During these rebellious, defiant, possibly hostile periods, parents are wise to give practical reasons for decisions. Once a reason is given, however, you certainly are not required to defend it like a doctoral thesis. Arguing with your teenager over the adequacy or legitimacy of the reason is seldom warranted. As long as the answer is reasonable, stating it simply is generally sufficient. Being willing to argue about it usually invites further disagreement and anger.

When our Carey wanted to date at age 12, we told her that she could not date until she was more mature, which we estimated to be in about four years. We left plenty of room for error. Remember, it is far better to be able to become less restrictive than to be forced to become more restrictive.

Carey asked, "Why not?" We explained to her that in this world it is extremely important to be able to function well in groups, and that the age when we learn to operate effectually in groups is early adolescence. There are many adults who never learned to function in groups when they were 12 to 14 years old and who consequently are "social misfits." Then I dramatically exclaimed, "And no daughter of mine is going to be a social misfit!" We told her that when she learned to function well in groups, then we would talk about other social privileges.

This worked for about a year. Then Carey came to her mother and me and stated she had learned to operate in groups. We told her she had indeed made good progress but that being able to function in groups was not simply getting along with everyone. It also meant offering a positive, constructive contribution to the group. It was not merely to be influenced by the group, but to have an influence on the group. We pointed out that she was making excellent progress, but that she was not yet a leader—that the other kids had more influence on her than she did on them. I'm happy to say that Carey increased her group leadership abilities and learned to have a warm, wholesome, gentle, but strong influence, not only in her church group but in her school and other organizations.

Protecting Your Teenager

Parents of teenagers need to be in good communication with parents of other teenagers—on a first-name basis, if you will—and especially with the parents of the teenagers who are closest to their own teen. It's a priceless asset to be able to share information and concerns with other parents and to work together with them in providing direction and control for the young people.

I can think of many occasions when Carey would be invited to a social event we knew nothing about. How grateful we were to be able to call different parents who were equally concerned and willing to check the appropriateness of a party.

How can parents know if a certain event is appropriate or not? Parents must not be hesitant about getting on the telephone and asking questions, no matter who is sponsoring the event. I'm sorry to say that many parents today are not only condoning immoral and destructive influences on youth but are actively encouraging them.

You should not be afraid to call the parent or adult sponsor to find out about planned activities. How else are you going to control and protect your vulnerable teen? And when you do call, listen carefully to the attitude or tone of what that person tells you since this usually conveys more than the actual words. For example, when the parent or adult sponsor actually sounds pleased and even thankful that you are calling regarding your teenager, that is a good sign. It's a wonderful thing to hear someone say how grateful he or she is that a parent cares enough about a child to find out what's going on. When I hear that, I thank God that there are still decent, loving, guiding parents in this world.

Unfortunately, however, you may receive a different response. I remember calling a mother who was giving a party to which Carey, then 15, was invited. This mother's response to my inquiry was hostile. She said, "This is a private party. Your daughter is invited and she can come or not. It's up to her, but what I do in my own home is my business!" From this response alone, I knew that her home was no place for any teenager.

But I pressed her for details. I said, "I see. But I'm concerned about my daughter, and I'd really appreciate it if you would fill me in on the details of your get-together." By now the mother was angry, but with persistence I was able to gather that the teenagers would be served wine and bloody marys in a sensually provocative atmosphere.

This is commonplace today. You can't sit back and assume your teenagers are experiencing wholesome influences simply because the activities may be "supervised." You need to work together with other parents to provide wholesome activities and also be able to keep each other informed of what is going on with your children. No one else will do that for you. So many influences today are not what you would want your teenager to be exposed to.

Appropriateness and Trust

Keep two things in mind as you control and train your teenager. First, allow privileges based upon the trust relationship. Second, try to make sure your teenager can handle the particular situation before you allow him or her to go.

While these may seem to be conflicting statements, they're not. Too many parents become confused at this point. They may use the trust relationship in deciding on a privilege but fail to check into the circumstances and suitability of the occasion. Checking into the appropriateness of the situation does not mean you do not trust your teenager. Even though a teenager is trustworthy, means well, and has fine intentions, there are still situations he or she may not have the maturity to handle. In these cases, you must protect your teenager.

In regard to the party to which Carey was invited, she was quite trustworthy—it was her genuine intention to act appropriately. But she was too young and immature at that time to handle such a heavy situation.

When I told Carey she could not go to this event, her natural reaction was, "Why not?" She carefully pointed out that her previous behavior had been exemplary, that she knew how to behave appropriately, that she definitely would do so, and that I could trust her. My reply to her was that she was absolutely right. I was truly proud of her and knew that I could trust her. However, I felt she was not yet ready or able to handle such a pressurized and difficult situation as this particular event. I pointed out that, although my own behavior had also been exemplary and I was trustworthy, I was also a normal person who likewise could be tempted. I could probably handle most any social situation. One evidence of this, which I was able to point out to Carey, was during my Navy days when I was required to supervise my division of sailors during their "happy hours" in striptease and topless bars. But even there, I had certain external restraints on me—such as being in a naval officer's uniform and being completely responsible for the welfare of my men.

Even with these difficult tests of character behind me, I, as well as anyone else, can be tempted beyond my endurance if I am not careful to control my life. So, why should I take the chance of ruining my integrity, character, marriage, spiritual fellowship, welfare of my children, and my life? I pointed out to Carey that this is one reason why I don't go to bars and discos. I trust myself, but I have no absolute guarantees that I can manage every temptation. I told her of a well-known minister who felt his calling was among patronizers of bars. I was not surprised to learn of his change of lifestyle, which made a mockery of his ministry and his marriage.

I was able to tell Carey that I truly trusted her because of her previous good behavior, but that there were certain situations she was not yet ready to handle—and some that any right-thinking person should avoid.

Delaying

Let's say you give your teenager privileges based on your trust relationship and also on the appropriateness of each situation. These criteria are spelled out to your teen so he or she knows why you are making your decisions and that you are trying not to be simply arbitrary. Yet this is not quite the whole picture, for frequently, these types of decisions will be difficult to make.

I remember a situation when Carey was 15. She was invited to spend the day on a large boat to swim during the day, then at night there would be a party aboard the boat. My wife and I were having some tough thoughts about this one. The day activities certainly seemed all right. But the thought of the party that night somehow bothered us. We knew the parents who would supervise the party were sensible people.

At this point, let me insert some good advice: If you ever get into a situation where you do not feel comfortable about an upcoming event that your teenager wants to go to—yet you can't put your finger on the reason why—your best response is to delay.

I usually say something like, "Wow, that's a tough one, Honey; let me think it over." In the teenager world, events and situations change so fast that this type of problem usually takes care of itself. I can think of only one or two occasions when the problem did not somehow resolve itself. Another advantage of delay is that your teenager will have time to think it over and may come to some mature decisions himself or herself. In the example of Carey being invited to the day and night party aboard the boat, I said, "Let me think it over." And Carey said, "OK, but hurry; I have to know by Thursday."

Much to my chagrin, the situation had not resolved itself. The questionable event was still on, the weather forecast was excellent, and it was Thursday evening already, with Carey saying in an irritated voice, "What's your answer, Daddy? Greg has to know tonight."

I had a terrible feeling in the pit of my stomach because I couldn't think of any legitimate reason to say no. Carey's behavior had been exemplary. Just as I was ready to give her permission to go, she said, "Daddy, by the way." (Remember those critical words?) "Greg can't get his folks' car to go to the party; we have to go in his dune buggy—you know, the one with no seat belts—and we have to cross the bridge during the five o'clock traffic."

I am surely glad I was listening closely at that moment, for I immediately responded, "I'm sorry, but you may not go to the party."

Carey did not even ask why, but went directly to the phone, called Greg and said, "I'm sorry; I can't go to the party. My father won't let me."

Many times, a teenager will give clues when he or she wants or needs a "No" to a question or privilege. You must listen closely for these clues, for they usually occur when your teenager needs a way out of a difficult peer situation. When he or she can use you as a defense or alibi in such a situation, this produces a wonderful sense of camaraderie between you and your teenager. You should permit your teenager to use you in this way. Of course, you must also be careful not to lie or allow your teen to be dishonest in accomplishing it.

As you can see in Carey's situation, she somehow sensed that she could not handle the boat party at that time and needed a way out. Perhaps it was her discomfort about it that made me uncomfortable. I really don't know. But at any rate, I am so thankful Carey took advantage of our parental authority and removed herself from a possibly unwholesome situation.

Looking Ahead

Let me tell you about another strategy I have found to be invaluable in dealing with the teenager's drive for independence and pressing for more freedom and privileges. The attitude of the parents toward their child's growth to responsible independence will strongly affect a teenager's response to control and authority.

If you approach your teenager with an attitude of keeping him or her dependent on you, perhaps out of fear, and attempting to actually stifle growth to independence, your child will react poorly. If your teenager yields to this type of attitude, he or she will be hampered in progressing to responsible adulthood and may become a passive, dependent person. If your child resists this overprotective attitude, his or her relationship with you will, of course, deteriorate and much conflict will result.

So what should your attitude and philosophy be? The most healthy attitude is to work hand-in-hand with your teenager toward being a responsible, independent person by the time he or she is at the legal age of adulthood. If you clearly state this so your teenager understands that you actually want him or her to be independent within a given time and are working toward that end, your teen can then feel you are for and not against him or her.

Teenagers need to be reminded of this partnership from time to time, especially when they want to go someplace that their parents feel is inappropriate. For example, let's say that your teenager wants to go to a party that you have checked out and feel is inappropriate. We'll assume you have done a good job in being available and in keeping your teenager's emotional tank full. Also, you have been using the trust relationship effectively in determining what privileges to give. And you have employed the delay technique, but the problem has not resolved itself. You find that you must now say no. And you find that your teenager simply will not or cannot accept it.

This is a good time to use the strategy I mentioned. I've found it to be very effective in helping teenagers gain perspective, to understand that their parents are working on their behalf and not trying to hold them back from gaining independence. In my experience, this difficult time seems to occur most frequently when teenagers are 16. They have recently gotten their driver's licenses, which feeds the urge for new experiences. How forceful you need to be with this strategy depends, of course, on the specific situation.

I remember counseling parents of a 16-year-old boy named Randy who was utterly determined to go to a concert that was obviously unwholesome. Up to that time, the parents had been able to control his behavior and social development fairly well by using the trust relationship and delay techniques. But this occasion was different. The parents had almost come to the point of letting Randy go. Of course, this would have been a mistake. We must remember that teenagers need parents to be in control at all times. It's all right for parents to change their minds for good reason, but not as capitulation to the teenager's demands.

I advised these fine parents to be pleasant but firm as they explained to Randy that they wanted him to become independent and be able to make his own decisions as soon as he was able. He was sixteen and a half, and they had only 18 months to make Randy a completely independent person. In only 18 months he would legally be an adult and after that date, he could be expected to handle his own affairs, make his own living, find his own place to live, do his own laundry, cooking, etc.

If these facts still do not give your teenager perspective (they do in the majority of cases), and he or she remains oppositional, you may go further and state that you have no legal responsibility after your child turns 18, that you intend to do everything in your parental power to get your child ready for adult life in the next 18 months because your legal responsibility ends at that time. Again, be sure to say "legal" to avoid regretting your words later because, of course, parents have other responsibilities to their children after they turn 18.

This strategy is a rather harsh thing to do to teenagers and should be used only as a last resort in difficult circumstances. However, teenagers need to be aware that the parents' overall intention is to indeed prepare them for responsible independence and adulthood, not to hold them back.

You can reinforce this attitude in several ways. For example, providing teenagers with their own checking accounts, placing monthly deposits into the accounts, and teaching them to be responsible for certain expenses is an excellent way to foster an attitude of cooperation between you and your teen in working toward independence. Initially, teenagers should be responsible for buying only a few items. As they learn to assume more responsibility, they can be given additional items to be responsible for, on a graduated scale, with the idea of becoming able by the age of 18 to assume total financial responsibility.

Another way to foster this attitude of working together in gaining independence in your teenager is, during times of good communication, to talk about the future, what he or she wants to do after high school, what vocation he or she might consider, whether college is right, and if so, which one. Looking at colleges with your teenager is a very effective means of fostering a feeling of cooperation. Providing any new experience for your teenager, such as a new sport or hobby, also helps accomplish this.

Setting Limits

A question parents frequently raise is how much restriction to impose on a teenager for misconduct. Teenagers, like all children, have an acute sense of fairness. They know when parents are permissive and when they are too harsh or unreasonable. I've seen parents on both ends of the spectrum. Some have extreme difficulty in consistently setting firm limits and are easily manipulated by their teenagers. Other parents take the opposite tack and impose harsh treatment. I know of one teenager who was restricted to her home for over a year for going to a bar. Parents need to remember that the punishment should fit the crime. Common sense must prevail! Lesser misbehavior, such as coming in 15 minutes late after a date, warrants restrictions of less than a week. If it recurs, then the restriction must be lengthened. Restrictions longer than two weeks are seldom warranted, with four weeks as an extreme outside limit. If restrictions are frequent, especially in ranges greater than one week, something is wrong—possibly in the parents' expectation, the parent-child relationship, or other possibilities we will discuss later.

Above all, remember that well-loved teenagers are so much easier to discipline and control than those who are not so loved. We must keep their emotional tanks full.

Parent Courtesy

Another point to be aware of is the great importance of parents being considerate and pleasant to their teenagers' peers. They should be cordial, regardless of their feelings toward them. Many needless problems arise as a direct result of parental hostility toward adolescent peers. Remember, parents are authority figures. Most teenagers will consequently pity and side with a peer who is being ill-treated by a parent, regardless of the situation.

One of the most tragic examples of this occurred in the Dempsey family. Jane dated a boy who upset her parents. He was several years older than Jane and was known to deal in drugs. He was also surly and disrespectful toward authority.

Due to several factors, one of the greatest being her parents' extremely hostile way of relating to the boy, Jane became more and more involved with him. Of course, this brought heartache to the parents.

Being civil to anyone, including your teenager's peers, definitely pays off. First of all, your teenager will appreciate it and can feel free to bring other teenagers home. Second, other teens often are having problems communicating with their parents. Many times they are seeking other adults to relate to in a positive way. It is a wonderful privilege to befriend your teenager's friends. Not only does this help them, but it draws your own teen closer to you.

Third, when you treat "unwholesome" peers kindly, you avoid pushing your teenager toward them, as the Dempseys did in Jane's case.

In fact, what usually happens is that your teenager will later approach you with questions regarding peers. Your teen will want your opinion about friends. Then your teenager will listen to your opinions. But if you are hostile toward your child's friends, your teenager usually will avoid discussing that issue with you, and you in turn will have lessened your influence on your child.

Abnormal Situations

What we have talked about thus far bears upon normal situations. However, there are times when parents are not facing normal problems. If a teenager, despite unconditional love and appeals to reason from parents, is continually difficult to manage, it's likely he or she has more serious problems and needs outside help.

There are several teenage behavioral problems parents may be unable to deal with. One of these is depression, which can be complex and treacherous on the teenage level. Another problem we are encountering more and more frequently is thought disorders, or difficulty in controlling one's thinking. Still another area that calls for professional help is neurological disorders with resultant emotional difficulties.

A physician needs to be aware of possible character disorders. One evidence of this is a teenager's inability to handle anger appropriately. Also, a teenager's behavior may be difficult to control because of problems in the family dynamics or relationships. In fact, a teenager's behavioral problems may be caused or aggravated by any combination of these factors. Since behavioral problems in teenagers are becoming more and more common and increasingly complex, a wise parent will seek help early before they become serious. Most problems can be handled effectively by competent, well-trained therapists, along with cooperation from the parents.

In recent years, professionals in education, medicine, and mental health have made great strides in the understanding of the complex problem known as attention deficit disorder (ADD) or attention deficit hyperactive disorder (ADHD). We have space here to cover only a few critical points.

First of all, I regret that these unfortunate children are considered abnormal. I have seen hundreds of these children, and they are not "abnormal." Almost all of them possess unique gifts but seldom are able to discover them because of problems with school, self-esteem, depression, or passive-aggressive behavior. These children are born with two basic "problems." One is "hyperactivity," which is simply a short-attention span. They have problems keeping their minds on a task in order to learn at their intellectual capacity.

Second, these young children and teenagers have "perceptual problems," which does not mean there is anything abnormal in their eyes or ears. Information is received by the brain, but as this information is processed in the brain, it becomes distorted. When the information comes to the child's awareness, it is not exactly what the child is seeing or hearing (and the distortion differs in each child).

We do not have the time or space here to explain the reasons in depth, but it's critical to know that these distorted perceptions cause ADD children to feel unloved and unwanted. Young children and teenagers with perceptual problems misperceive feelings received from others just as they misperceive academic data. Unfortunately, ADD children perceive our feelings for them negatively. It's therefore difficult to make an ADD child feel genuinely loved and cared for. This, in turn, causes increasing depression and anger as the child grows older. Eventually, the depression and anger (which is primarily manifested in passive-aggressive behavior) become so strong that they become the child's (and parents') greatest problems. These can occur at any age, but usually the depression becomes serious around the age of 10, and the passive-aggressive behavior becomes a worsening problem as the child enters adolescence. At this time normal adolescent passive-aggressive behavior is superimposed on the PA behavior derived from the ADD, and these children are prone to a very difficult adolescence. God, help these children and their parents.

From the above, I hope that you can see how critical it is to understand that ADD kids are normal but are nonetheless prone to special problems with depression and passive-aggressive behavioral traits that eventually make hyperactivity and learning disabilities pale in comparison. Unfortunately, most ADD children receive only special education and medication in the way of help. Appropriate and carefully managed special education and medication may be beneficial, but the far more important and potentially devastating depression and passive-aggressive behavior are largely ignored.

If you have a child with ADD or ADHD, please be assured that if your teenager receives what he or she needs, the prognosis is good to excellent that your child will eventually do well. Remember, this is a long process because it is a developmental process. Keep providing what your teenager needs daily. In general, here is what you must do:

1. Study, learn, and understand all you can about ADD.

2. Realize that your ADD child is not abnormal but is prone to certain problem areas. Remember, no child is perfect.

3. Please read and reread—even memorize—chapter 9 on adolescent depression. Otherwise, you are likely to miss it if and when your ADD child becomes depressed and needs help. If depression reaches the moderate range, seek professional help as soon as possible.

4. This may sound extreme, but please read chapters 6 and 7 every night for a week before you fall asleep. Handling a teenager's anger is the most difficult part of child-rearing in my opinion. If you read chapters 6 and 7 one time, you will probably do well for a few days but gradually fall back to reacting to your teenager's anger in inappropriate ways. So please read these chapters nightly with the determination to maintain the correct "mind-set" for the next 24 hours. You must remain consistent.

5. Remember, it is quite difficult to make an ADD teenager feel genuinely loved. We must apply the basic ways of loving a child (eye contact, physical contact, focused attention, and loving discipline) with extreme diligence to accomplish this. Also remember that corporal punishment is easily misinterpreted by an ADD child or teen as violence, which he or she then uses to justify violence.

9

Adolescent Depression

Adolescent depression is a complex, subtle, and dangerous phenomenon. It's complex because of its many seemingly unrelated causes and effects. It's subtle because it almost always goes undiagnosed and undetected—even by teenagers who experience it— until a tragedy occurs. It's dangerous because depression can result in the worst of happenings—from school failure to suicide.

Over the years, I've seen many teenagers who have attempted to harm or kill themselves. Usually, their parents and friends are stunned and shocked in disbelief at the action. These distressed people believed that everything was well with their teenagers, never guessing that they were so unhappy.

Teenage depression is difficult to identify because its symptoms are different from the classical symptoms of adult depression. For example, a teenager in mild depression acts and talks normally. There are no outward signs of depression. Mild teenage depression is manifested in somber fantasies, daydreams, or dreams during sleep. Mild depression is detectable only by somehow knowing the teen's thought pattern and thought content. Few professionals are able to pick up depression in this state.

In moderate depression too, a depressed teenager acts and talks normally. However, in moderate depression, the content of the teenager's speech is affected, dwelling primarily on depressing subjects such as death, morbid problems, and crises. Since many adults today seem to dwell on pessimistic trains of thought, even a teenager's moderate depression may go unnoticed.

Some years ago, an anxious mother called me regarding her 14-year-old son. She was not sure if her son needed help. This loving mother said her boy was acting normally, looked normal, and talked normally—that everything seemed fine except that after watching the news he would say something like this: "Things are getting so bad in the world, I wonder if it would be better to be dead." This fine boy was found to be moderately depressed.

Moderate depression in adults can be quite crippling. It can cause severe sleeping and eating problems and inability to function in various capacities, from parenting to vocation. It may lead to serious consequences, even suicide.

Moderate depression in teenagers is just as profound and serious as in adults. Biochemically and neurohormonally, the two are essentially identical. But you see how different the manifestations or symptoms are. A moderately depressed adult usually looks terrible, feels miserable, and is severely affected in ability to function. But a teenager? In the vast majority of cases, only in severe depression does a teenager actually appear depressed. When we can say, "Boy, does that kid look depressed!" we should assume that particular teenager is profoundly depressed and probably suicidal.

There is an exception to this, however. Teenage depression is difficult to identify because teens are good at "masking" it; that is, they can cover it by appearing OK even when they are absolutely miserable. This is often called "smiling depression." This is a front teenagers employ unconsciously. They mask depression primarily when other people are around. When depressed teenagers are alone, they let down or relax the mask.

This is helpful to parents. If we are able to see our teenagers at times when they believe no one is looking at them, we may be able to identify depression. It's an amazing thing to see the transformation in the face. Alone they will appear terribly sad and miserable.

As soon as they think someone is watching, the smiling mask immediately appears as though nothing is wrong.

Discovering Depression

How, then, can we discover depression in a teenager so that we can do something about it before tragedy occurs? It's imperative that we be able to identify it early since there are numerous ways today that depression can bring harm to our children. A depressed teenager is quite susceptible to unhealthy peer pressure, is prone to fall victim to drugs, alcohol, criminal activity, inappropriate sexual experiences, and other antisocial behaviors, including suicide.

The best way to identify depression in a teenager is to understand the various symptoms manifested in teenage depression and how they develop. It is crucial to understand the total constellation of symptoms in detail because one or two symptoms may or may not signify true depression. True depression is a biochemical and neurohormonal process that in teenagers usually develops slowly over a period of weeks or months.

Before we consider the specific symptoms of adolescent depression, we should understand that a depressed adolescent may also have one or more of the classic symptoms of adult depression, including feelings of helplessness, hopelessness, despondency, and despair; problems with sleep (either too much or too little); problems with eating (too much or too little with weight loss or gain); lack of energy; feelings of low self-worth; problems handling anger.

Now let's look at the more specific symptoms of adolescent depression:

1. Shortened attention span. In mild teenage depression, the first visible symptom generally is a shortening of attention span. The teenager is not able to keep focused on a subject very long. The mind drifts from what he or she wants to focus on, and the teen becomes increasingly distractable and daydreams more and more. This shortening of attention span usually becomes obvious when the teen attempts homework. The teen finds it harder and harder to keep focused on it. And it seems that the harder the teenager tries, the less he or she accomplishes. Of course, this leads to frustration, as the teenager then blames himself or herself for being "stupid" or "dumb." He assumes that he doesn't have the intellectual ability to do the work. Imagine what this does to his self-esteem.

2. Daydreaming. The shortened attention span affects the teenager in the classroom. At first, he may be able to pay attention to the classwork for most of the period and then daydream the remaining minutes. As the depression deepens and the attention span becomes shorter, the teenager pays attention less and daydreams more. At this point, a teacher is in the best position to identify symptoms of depression. Unfortunately, daydreaming is usually interpreted as laziness or poor attitude. However, just one or two symptoms alone, such as daydreaming and short attention span, do not allow a person to make the diagnosis of true adolescent depression. We must see a gradual development of an array of symptoms.

3. Poor grades. As the teenager's attention span shortens and daydreaming increases, the natural result is lower grades. Unfortunately, falling grades is usually so gradual that it is difficult to notice. For this reason, it's seldom associated with depression. In fact, the teenager, the parents, and the teacher usually assume that the work is too difficult for the teenager or that the teen is becoming more interested in other things. It would be quite helpful if the grades took a drastic plunge, an A to a D in one grading period, for instance. This would arouse the appropriate concern. However, the grades usually go something like this: A, A-, B+, B. Therefore, depression is seldom considered.

4. Boredom. As the teenager daydreams more and more, he or she gradually falls into a state of boredom. Boredom is normal in teenagers, especially in early adolescence, but only for relatively short periods of time. Normal boredom is frequently seen for an hour or two, sometimes for an entire evening or day, or occasionally even two days. But prolonged boredom, several days or more, is not normal and should be a warning that something is not right. Few things worry me as much as prolonged boredom in an adolescent, especially an early adolescent. Boredom usually manifests itself by teenagers wanting to stay alone in their rooms for increasingly longer periods of time. They spend this time just lying on the bed, daydreaming and listening to music. Bored teenagers lose interest in things they once enjoyed, for example, sports, clothes, cars, hobbies, clubs, church and social activities, and dating.

5. Somatic depression. As the boredom continues and deepens, the teenager gradually slips into moderate depression. At this point, he or she begins to suffer from what I call somatic depression. I use this term because, even though all depression is physiological, or has a bio-chemical-neurohormonal basis, at this point the symptoms begin to affect the child in a directly physical way. For example, in moderate depression, the teenager begins to experience physical pain. This pain may occur in many places, but most often in the lower mid-chest region or as headaches. Many teenagers suffer pain in the lower chest or head, secondary to depression.

6. Withdrawal. In this miserable state, the teenager may withdraw from peers. And to make matters worse, he or she doesn't simply avoid peers but may disengage from them with such hostility, belligerence, and unpleasantness that he or she alienates them. As a result, the teenager becomes very lonely. When teens have so thoroughly antagonized good friends, they find themselves associated with rather unwholesome peers who may use drugs or are frequently in trouble. The situation becomes more frightening.

Once prolonged boredom has set in, many things can develop. The mental and physical pain at this stage may be excruciating and at times unbearable. A teenager at this stage cannot tolerate misery indefinitely. Eventually, he or she becomes desperate enough to do something about this misery. Most amazingly, even at this point the teenager is hardly ever aware that he or she is depressed. The teenager's ability to hide behind denial is truly incredible. This is why depression is seldom suspected until tragedy occurs.

Acting Out Depression
When a teenager has been moderately to severely depressed to the extent that he can endure it no longer, he will take action in an

attempt to alleviate his misery and distress. The teenager's action resulting from depression is termed "acting out depression." There are many ways for a teenager to act out depression.

Boys tend to be more violent than girls. Boys may attempt to relieve their depressive symptoms by stealing, lying, fighting, driving fast, or through other types of antisocial behavior. One of the most common kinds of criminal behavior seen today among boys is breaking and entering. Doing something with an air of excitement and danger seems to relieve the pain of depression. Breaking into homes provides this air; therefore, depressed boys commonly resort to it.

Of course, boys break into homes for other reasons. So when a teenager is referred to me for behavior such as breaking and entering, one of my first concerns is to find how much depression has played into the teenager's behavior. This is critical because a depressed teenager generally does not respond well to help if the depression is not treated as well. I believe that overlooking the depression in these young people is completely negligent. And unfortunately, most agencies dealing with teens focus on behavior and are unaware of the depressive component in each child's problem.

Girls tend to act out their depression in less violent ways. However, because of unhealthy, violence-oriented models in the media, this trend is changing. Girls frequently act out their depression by sexual promiscuity. Their depressive pain tends to be alleviated during the close physical relationship of intercourse. However, when the relationship is over, these unfortunate girls usually feel worse—more depressed—than before because of the self-degradation involved. Depression and low self-esteem are almost always the basis of a girl's promiscuity. It's amazing how much we can help a girl with this type of problem by taking care of her depression. It's equally true how little we can do if we neglect her depression.

A depressed teenager can also act out depression by taking drugs. Marijuana and depression are a very dangerous combination because marijuana actually makes a depressed teenager feel better. Marijuana is not an antidepressant. Rather, it blocks the pain of depression. Unfortunately, the teenager feels better simply because he or she does not hurt as much. Of course, when the marijuana is out of the system, the depressive pain returns. Then in order to obtain the same degree of relief from the pain, the teenager must use a greater quantity. This is a common way for a teenager to become habituated to marijuana, to become a "pothead." Other drugs can affect a depressed teenager in the same way. So naturally, when we attempt to help a teenager on drugs, we must determine how great a role depression is playing in his or her drug usage. I am genuinely alarmed how depression is overlooked or discounted by many professionals and agencies involved in treating adolescent drug problems.

Another way a depressed teenager may act out depression is by attempting suicide. Sometimes the attempt is a gesture; the teenager does not wish death, but attention. At other times, the attempt to die is genuine. Girls make many more suicide attempts than boys, but boys are more often successful in killing themselves. Girls generally use less violent means of attempting suicide, such as pills. Boys, on the other hand, use more violent means, such as guns. Of course, this makes it easier to save girls from their own attempts. However, I have seen many girls come extremely close to death or actually die. What a tragedy!

Remedy for Mild Depression

What can we do to help depressed teenagers? First of all, we must identify depression early in order to prevent tragedy. This means we must be familiar with symptoms of adolescent depression. People who need this information most are parents and those who work with teenagers, such as teachers, school counselors, and youth workers. When the depression is mild, it's relatively easy to halt its insidious progress and alleviate it.

Although most adolescent depression is complex in its underlying causes, often a specific factor or event finally overwhelms the child and triggers the constellation of symptoms. This includes, for example, a death or illness, or departure of a person important to the teenager, a disappointment such as a divorce or conflict between parents, or a move to an undesired place. In such situations, the teenager feels lonely, abandoned, and unloved. It's crucial, first of all, to show we do care about and love the teen. We show this by spending enough time with the teen to permit psychological defenses to come down in order for the teenager to be able to meaningfully communicate with us. Then our love-giving, that is, eye contact, physical contact, and focused attention, will be meaningful.

If the problem is a conflict within the family, for example a divorce, teenagers need help in dealing with their own feelings about this. They especially need to realize that the divorce is not their fault and that there was nothing they could have done to prevent it.

Teenagers are extremely sensitive to problems between their parents. Unfortunately, most people seem to believe that once teenagers finish high school and leave home, they are not really affected by what happens between parents. How utterly wrong this is.

I remember the first time we visited our daughter Carey after she went away to college. We went with about 20 of her friends for a snack one evening. All of Carey's friends were freshmen, away from home for the first time. All of them stated how much they loved school, their new friends, and college life, but they also voiced distress that they received so little communication from their parents. Few phone calls, letters, or visits.

Most parents simply do not realize how traumatic this period is in a young person's life and how important it is to continue to provide a solid, stable "home base." About the worst time for parents to divorce is around the time the teenager leaves home. Going away from home, especially for the first time, is one of the most unsettling, anxiety-provoking, and insecure parts of anyone's life. At that time, a teenager's primary foundation of security is in parents and home. Divorce at that time utterly shatters these sources of teenage stability. But it's amazing how naive so many people are and how many parents have divorced right after their children have gone off to college. This has a profound effect on the teenager's value system, undermining faith in the sanctity of marriage. It leaves little opportunity to resolve feelings of frustration, anger, anxiety, rejection, and fear regarding parents before teenagers themselves consider marriage. Some of this unresolved inner conflict may affect their own marriages and cause conflict with spouses.

Moderate and Severe Depression

As depression deepens within teenagers, a serious complication develops. Their thought process begins to be affected. In moderate and severe depression, teenagers gradually lose their ability to think clearly, logically, and rationally. Their judgment deteriorates as they lose the ability to maintain healthy perspective, and they focus more and more on morbid, depressing details. Their perceptions of reality become distorted, especially concerning what they perceive other people are thinking about them. More and more they assume that everything is bleak, nothing is worthwhile, and life is not worth living.

The teenager now has a thought disturbance. As the teenager increasingly loses the ability to think and communicate in a clear, rational way, counseling per se becomes less and less effective. This is a frightening predicament. How can you help a teenager in counseling when you cannot reason with him or her? When this situation occurs, medical help is mandatory. For it's usually when the teenager loses the ability to be rational, reasonable, and logical that he or she begins to act out depression in self-destructive ways.

Adolescent depression is not something you can consider a phase that will run its course. This insidious affliction tends to grow worse and worse unless the depression is identified and intervention is taken.

Depression and Drugs

A depressed teenager is quite susceptible to drug usage because many drugs, especially marijuana, block or dull the pain of depression. It's also amazing how many teenagers and adults actually believe that marijuana is harmless. Every day we see the effect of this subtly hazardous drug.

I recall admitting a 15-year-old boy to the hospital for drug abuse, severe depression, and behavioral problems. Included in our initial evaluation, of course, were the physician's examinations and blood tests. I found this child to be severely anemic. His body was gradually losing its ability to manufacture blood due to drug abuse. Before treating this youngster for his psychological problems, I had to transfer him to a university medical center for a blood marrow transplant. His prognosis was very poor.

All this leads back to parental control of a teenager's freedom by allowing privileges and freedoms based on trust and trustworthiness and on the appropriateness of the activity. If your teenager genuinely feels that you love and care about him, he will likely listen to you and heed your advice regarding his safety. Therefore, you must keep your teen's emotional tank full. Then you will be able to help your child avoid harmful consequences of yielding to peer pressure to use drugs. You must continue to remind your teenager not to carelessly drink or eat something without being sure that no one has slipped a drug into the drink or food. At any questionable party, it's good common sense for your teenager to avoid open punch bowls or accepting food and drink from someone he or she doesn't know well. This may sound overly suspicious, but I have personally seen how a single ingestion of a drug can harm a teen's developing mind.

The most frightening aspect of drugs is the way they affect a teenager's thought process. I have seen numerous teenagers who could not think sequentially or logically even after one dose of drugs. This disturbance of thought process is often so subtle that no one detects it, but the results are devastating. Teenagers' ability to relate positively to people deteriorates. They come up with wrong and often bizarre ideas about people, values, authority, society, and themselves. They misinterpret people and their motivations. Worst of all, because they cannot think clearly, they becomes somewhat confused and easily led by peer groups, cults, and other people interested only in using them.

What is more frightening than people who cannot think accurately and have distorted ideas, distorted views, and distorted values? Are you willing to make sure your teenager gets through adolescence without his or her intellectual, social, and psychological assets being harmed or destroyed? If so, you will love your teenager. Take close care to appropriately supervise. It's a difficult job, but the reward is well worth the cost. Seeing your teenager develop into a mature, sensitive, independent, right-thinking adult contributing to the world is one of life's greatest rewards.

10

Helping Your Teenager Intellectually

*To prepare your adolescent for the future in this world of non-*reason, you must teach him or her to think clearly. There are five basic reasons for this.

First, your teen needs clear thinking for a basic understanding of the world the way it is. Adolescents do not have a historical perspective and cannot understand daily events without logical reasoning.

Second, a teen must learn to think clearly to understand the difference between right and wrong. Without a sound, rational understanding of ethics, a teenager is easy prey to antiauthority, destructive attitudes so prevalent today. Observe the ethical and moral tone of so many influential personalities in entertainment, government, and religious life today. We must arm our teens against destructive influences. This is not easy to do as we see most adults today become increasingly confused and bewildered. Inappropriate, unethical behavior is rapidly becoming the norm in our society.

Third, we must train teenagers to think clearly to enable them to make logical, rational decisions for themselves. We want their behavior to be based on good decision-making and sound reasoning. Too much behavior in our society today is not based on careful, rational thought but on irrational, impulsive whims. We live in an antiauthority society due to the immature handling of anger (see chapter 7), and the tide is worsening. A clear-thinking person has a vast advantage.

Fourth, clear thinking enables teens to develop socially and become socially mature adults. The person who has the ability to be rational and to think logically in his or her dealings with different types of people and personality styles is a rare but fortunate individual. Naturally, this gift will strongly influence the teen to develop a decent, positive, strong character.

Fifth, without logical, clear thinking, a teen cannot have a strong, consistent, lasting faith or a moral value system. A faith that is solid and enduring and provides the basis for life's meaning cannot be a blind faith. It must be based on rational, logical reason. It must be consistent with the real world. And it must provide reasonable answers to life's deepest questions.

It's very important that you teach your teenager to think rationally, logically, and sequentially (keeping facts in proper order). One of the best pieces of armament you can give teenagers is the ability to evaluate their own thinking so that they can have confidence in it and be able to modify it in light of new knowledge. In addition, they should learn to see errors in faulty thinking and understand how false conclusions are reached. How do you help your teenager do this?

Intellectual Development

A child develops intellectually from one phase to another. The factor that most determines how well a child masters each stage of thought development is the degree of emotional nourishment he or she receives. The better job you do in unconditionally and genuinely loving your teen, the better able he or she will be to develop intellectually. The more teens feel loved, the more they will be able to learn to think clearly and logically. The less teens feel loved and cared for, the weaker their minds may be.

For their minds to grow in a strong, healthy manner, teenagers must first feel good about themselves. Then they will be able to mature into wise and understanding persons who can maintain proper perspective, especially over their emotions. The young person who is not emotionally well nourished may have poor thought control and be overcome and over controlled by feelings. You must meet your teenager's emotional needs first.

Some years ago I counseled a muscularly built 14-year-old boy who had attacked his baseball coach with a bat. The boy felt totally justified in his act. He maintained he had the right to attack his coach because he and the coach's son were competing for the same position, and he thought he was at a disadvantage.

The poor reasoning that this boy expressed is called loose association. By using loose association in the thought process, a person can justify almost anything. Such confused thinking is illogical and dangerous. And it is becoming more and more common among our teenagers today. Unfortunately, this faulty thought process is subtle and difficult to identify in casual relationships. But it is one of the primary reasons many of our teens are not being prepared for mature adult life.

You should constantly be alert for opportunities to teach your teenager to make correct, accurate associations in thinking. A typical adolescent cannot think abstractly to a significant degree until he is at least 15 years old, and then he is just learning. This is why a teenager is often sure parents are wrong or ignorant during early and middle adolescence; later, as the thought process matures and the teen becomes capable of abstract reasoning, he or she begins to understand parents and respect their opinions.

You need to be patient and loving during these difficult times and gently train your teenager to think clearly. And one way to do this is to identify faulty association of ideas and correct it.

Intellectual Affirmation

A teenager needs intellectual affirmation to learn to think well. To be able to think creatively, a person must respect himself, not only emotionally and physically but also intellectually. He must feel approval regarding his ability to think. This does not mean giving the impression that you believe your teen is always right. It is, rather, encouraging your child in a growing self-respect for his or her ability to reason and solve problems.

Most teenagers cannot feel this self-assurance and self-approval without first receiving assurance and approval from their parents or parent figures. Many parents make the mistake of only correcting their teenagers. But a teen will feel competent only if he or she receives approval, validation, and praise, as well as correction.

You can give these priceless assets to teenagers only if you engage them intellectually. This means being available to discuss with them any subject they want to talk about. It means being willing to listen to their ideas and to fully hear them out, regardless of your own reaction. Then, instead of directly pointing out their mistakes or arguing with them, you can discuss the issues with respect, seriously considering their viewpoint and calmly expressing your own. Such conversation should resemble talk between good friends. In doing this, you are not giving up your parental authority. You are simply showing respect for your teenager's thinking. You are letting them know that their thoughts and opinions are worthy and valuable. If your teens feel that you love and respect them, they will gradually incorporate some of your opinions and values into their thinking.

Unfortunately, too many parents refuse to talk with their teenagers in a give-and-take manner. Instead, they persist in talking down to their teenagers as though they were small children. This makes teens feel that their opinions don't matter. They are not being intellectually affirmed. They are not feeling genuinely loved by their parents. They do not feel respected, and they become hurt and angry.

Add to this the fact that they have not learned whether their thinking is correct or incorrect, logical or irrational. They have had no feedback from parents about whether their ideas are meaningful.

Most teenagers do not know if they are right or wrong about the subjects they think about. This pushes them toward taking the opinions of others, who may not have their welfare at heart. When they become too alienated from family to accept the opinions and values of parents and other legitimate authority figures, they begin listening to people who desire to harm them mentally, emotionally, physically, or spiritually.

Make sure your teenager feels unconditionally loved, through use of eye contact, physical contact, and focused attention. Give intellectual affirmation by listening and carefully noticing the way he or she thinks and comes to conclusions. Respect your teen by giving your opinion without criticizing or denouncing your child's thinking.

Only when teenagers see that you are willing to relate to them as responsible persons with minds of their own will they feel a balanced confidence in their ability to learn to think clearly and grow to intellectual maturity.

When you criticize your teen's opinions, he or she probably will feel angry, resentful, and even bitter. And your child may become more defiant and resistant to change. If this happens, a teenager will hold to immature, selfish, and incorrect opinions, and carry these into his adult life. We all know adults who believe incorrect and strange ideas. These unfortunate people have difficulty understanding social, spiritual, or emotional relationships. They tend to jump on the current bandwagon and often hold unrealistic and antagonistic opinions.

Teach by Example

As a parent, I've made my share of mistakes. So it certainly has its advantages to be the writer of this book because I can choose the illustrations I wish to share. Let me give you one example that involves the intellectual training of our son David as he grew up. I think I handled this situation correctly as I attempted, without criticizing him, to show him where his thinking was illogical and too simplistic, and then to teach him more mature ways of thinking.

David knew which TV programs his mother and I approved of and which ones we didn't. And he was usually quite good in complying with our wishes regarding his TV viewing. One evening, however, he was watching a program we didn't like. When I reminded David that I did not want him to watch it, he asked,

"Why not?" and then said he could see nothing wrong with it because "no one is hurting anyone."

Does this reasoning sound familiar? Though he said it years ago, David's statement exemplifies the current state of morality in our society: "I can do what I want as long as it doesn't hurt anyone else."

It was very tempting for me to jump on David and criticize him for this shallow and immature way of thinking. TV programs then and more so now expose young people to subtle and dangerous philosophies. But I'm glad to report that I remembered that David needed intellectual affirmation and training to learn to think maturely.

So I said, "I understand what you mean, David, but I think this show is hedonistic and narcissistic." (That got his attention.)

He replied, "What does that mean?"

I said, "Tell you what, David. Let's get a dictionary and look these words up." (Incidentally, using the dictionary was a tremendous help to me in teaching my children difficult concepts.)

We looked the words up together. Then we talked about the meaning of hedonistic and narcissistic until I was sure he understood them. But, like a typical, developing early adolescent, after David understood the definitions, he still didn't understand how they related to real life. I said, "David, do you think a hedonistic and narcissistic person could make a good husband, wife, mother, or father? How about your mother? Is she selfish? Does she care only about herself with little regard for others? Is she only concerned about her own pleasure and not in anyone else's welfare?" This certainly turned on a light in David's head. He thought about all the things his loving mother had done for him that day even though she did not feel well.

I was overjoyed when David finally replied, "This means that a selfish person is interested only in getting pleasure for himself instead of caring about other people."

Then David and I talked about how the show's characters displayed selfish, self-gratifying attitudes with little regard for the respect or welfare of the other person.

Teaching a teenager to think clearly is difficult, time-consuming, and tedious. But if you do not clarify issues, such as those just described, those attitudes will subtly influence your teenager.

Be Consistent

One reason teenagers are confused about moral issues is that many parents are not assuming responsibility for teaching their own convictions to their children. Other parents say they believe in spiritual values, but they do not live them. Many parents—including Christians—are having difficulty with their own behavior. The rise in sexual misconduct, child abuse, and cheating is alarming.

Nothing is more confusing to a teenager than inconsistency in the life of the parent—especially about matters that the parents say they highly value and then treat as less than nothing. How can parents teach their teenagers to think clearly about moral and spiritual values if their own lives do not demonstrate the results of clear thinking?

I believe that the undisciplined behavior destroying the moral fiber of our society must be dealt with. Surely God will judge us for the lack of discipline and self-control in the lives of so many who call themselves Christians.

Fellow parents, let's get our own lives in order, consistently behaving as we know God wants us to. Then we can claim God's promises to us for our children.

11

Helping Your Teenager Spiritually

Today's generation of teenagers is often called the "antiauthority" or "apathetic generation." It's important to remember that this apathy and antiauthority attitude are coverings for intense anger and rage, especially toward legitimate authority. Unfortunately, many teenagers *are* apathetic, especially about the future. Many of these young people, who are the future hope of our country and way of life, lack the vitality, vivaciousness, and eagerness that we love to see.

Why are so many of adolescents apathetic? Why do they lack initiative and incentive? Why are so many of them poorly motivated? There are two principle reasons. The first is immature ways of handling anger. The other is that they have little hope in the future. Such feelings of resentment and hopelessness are more serious than the aggressive and violent protests of the late 1960s. Although the young people of those years had a cause that was at times misdirected and poorly carried out, they at least had a cause that reflected a hope—a hope in their country, in their way of life, and most importantly in themselves.

We do not see this today. The prevailing mood in our young today is feelings of resenting authority, hopelessness, helplessness, and despair. As parents, we wonder how this heartbreaking situation can be possible. It seems as if the very heart and soul have been torn from so many of our precious teenagers. Why do they have so little hope in the future?

It's easy to point out the disheartening world and national developments, such as unemployment, disasters, AIDS, world hunger, and pollution. But these are not the cause of teenage hopelessness and despair. Our forefathers faced equally difficult, dangerous, and frustrating times in the past and with even less security. They faced such hardships as the Great Depression, the Holocaust, and other horrors of World War II. But the young people of those eras did not feel the hopelessness and despair we see today.

The attitudes and moods of a nation's youth reflect the attitudes and moods of its adults. Sometimes the youth rally behind their elders, especially when national security is threatened. At other times, the young people march against the status quo, especially when they perceive hypocrisy. But today we see neither pro nor con, but rather a foreboding inertia. What are our youth reflecting from adults? They are reflecting depression, gloom, hopelessness, and despair. How can a teenager react positively in such an atmosphere? A teen needs to see something positive and worthwhile in life to rally behind.

Unfortunately, teenagers have little historical perspective to allow them to look back and learn from the experiences of their forebears. They are limited to the present and future. Therefore, they form their attitudes and moods from the current, prevailing climate of the present and the current, prevailing attitudes about the future.

One of the main reasons teenagers have problems forming positive attitudes is that adults are not passing on to them the determination, hope, and encouragement necessary for facing the future. We of the older generation seem to be offering our young people some strange and unhealthy attitudes that are largely untrue and certainly not Scriptural. Almost without realizing it, we are rapidly developing an orientation to life that is unwholesome, noncreative, retreating, and passive. We have let other people determine our value systems and outlook on life. Many of us believe:

- that we are the first generation to face crises;

- that the world was somehow a nicer, better, and safer place to live before the present problems developed;

- that the world is deteriorating so rapidly that it is hopeless and foolish to plan and prepare for the future since there may not be a future at all.

You could rightly expect a teenager, who knows little about the history of man and less about the great promises of God, to succumb to this suffocating, hope-robbing pessimism. We have become a people whose attitudes and value systems are so easily influenced by others. We feel despair when something is not as good as it once was, ignoring the things that are good. We forget to count our blessings. I've seen people despair over the most inconsequential things. On the other hand, we overreact positively to equally unimportant things, such as a new car or new clothes. Why should we think it strange that our young are so easily influenced by rock groups and cults when we are equally influenced by television and special interest groups?

I can understand a nonbeliever feeling this disorientation, confusion, and despair. But I find it difficult to understand the Christian person being in this trap of hopelessness. Yet I see so many Christians yielding to pessimistic influences. And I see their teenagers failing to find that critical peace-giving anchor of hope that Christ intends for his people.

I would like our teenagers to receive messages of hope, encouragement, and challenge. But the generation of their parents has generally lost contact with its spiritual heritage. Yes, we have problems, some of which are completely new—but so did many of our grandfathers and grandmothers. Why can't we face our crises and difficulties without foreboding, depression, without feelings of hopelessness and doom?

Doomsday?

In times of trouble, some religious groups and teachers have tried to escape responsibility by withdrawing and waiting for doomsday. Instead of using biblical passages as God intended—as words of hope and promise—these self-proclaimed prophets use the Scriptures to pronounce an imminent doomsday. Their message is one of hopelessness: The end is coming soon, so there is no point in solving our problems or providing a better life for our children. This results in a state of spiritual and emotional paralysis. It also encourages the attitude, "Eat, drink, and be merry, for tomorrow we die."

Imagine being an adolescent in such an atmosphere. At the time when a teenager should be preparing for a life of accomplishment to contribute to the world, he or she senses that the general attitude is to make the best of today because tomorrow, even if it comes, may not be worth living.

Such preoccupations are breaking the back of responsibility in both adolescents and adults. After reading a book on the "end times" recently offered on TV, one mother admitted, "I can't help wondering why I should raise my kids or try to prepare them for a nonexistent future." A man who read another doomsday book stated, "I feel like giving up my job and just quitting. Why go on?"

In this atmosphere of escalating futility, it's difficult for people to fight cynicism, to avoid drugs, or to keep from copping out. When doomsday is proclaimed without the proper balance of hope and trust in God's promises and Christ's love, is it any wonder that Christians find it increasingly difficult to live responsible, courageous, and productive lives?

Periods of unhealthy overemphasis on prophecy and end times occur every five to ten years. These periods are usually precipitated by a best-selling book on this subject that takes current conditions and compares them with biblical prophecy. This can have a devastating effect on a teenager. If and when this occurs, be ready to equip your teenager with an understanding of the history of this phenomenon and keep it in balance with sound understanding of biblical prophecy. Otherwise, teenagers cannot only become pessimistic and depressed about their existence but also may easily be drawn into astrology and fall under the growing influence of psychics, seers, and fortunetellers.

Pessimism is not the teaching of Christ. his message is one of hope and joy. Speaking of the last days, Christ said, "No one knows about that day or hour, not even the angels in heaven, nor the Son, but only the Father. Be on guard! Be alert! You do not know when that time will come" (Mark 13:32–33, NIV). We are to watch for his coming and to pray. We are not to give up or be pessimistic about the future. We are not to withdraw from our moral responsibility to live godly lives and to pass our values on to our children. The Scriptures encourage us to be joyful, optimistic, hopeful, and to assume the best.

If we as parents can grasp the total picture of history, we will see our place in it—a place of extreme importance and excitement. We are only one chapter in God's plans and books of history. And his plans and history will never end. When our chapter is over, I for one want to look back and know that we as his people have carried out his will, that we have stood firm in our faith in him and in his goodness. I want to feel good about not giving in to the world's pressures to use our resources for "experiences" today at the expense of sacrificing our God-given privilege to live righteous, godly lives. I want to be able to say with Paul, "I have fought the good fight, I have finished the race, I have kept the faith" (2 Tim. 4:7, NIV).

God help us to finish our course and keep the faith! For to do this to the best of our ability will give more to our teenagers than anything else. But to give our teenagers hope, faith, and optimism, we must live it.

"Show Me How to Live"

One of the main cries of adolescents today is for their parents to provide ethical and moral value systems to guide them. Teenagers express this in various ways. One child states he wants a "standard to live by." Another teenager needs a "meaning in life." Other teens long for "something to show me how to live" or "something to hold on to" or "a higher guidance."

These desperate yearnings are not experienced by only a few discontented, unhappy youngsters. Most teenagers feel these needs and are confused, so terribly confused, in this all-important area of their lives. Unfortunately, it is quite unusual to find teenagers who sense meaning and purpose in their lives, who are at peace with themselves, and who have a healthy perspective about living in a confusing, rapidly changing, and frightening world.

Initially, a child looks to his parents for guidance in life. Whether the child is successful in finding this from parents depends on two things: whether the parents have found direction for themselves and whether the child can accept parental values and make them his or her own. A child who is not able to feel genuinely loved by parents will find this difficult.

Let's examine the first requirement in providing the meaning to life a young person so desperately needs. Parents need a foundation on which to base their own lives, one that can stand the test of time, a foundation that will see us through every part of life, through marital needs, money crises, problems with our children, energy shortages, and clashes within a changing society where spiritual standards are rapidly weakening. Parents must possess that foundation to be able to pass it on to their children.

This priceless, comfort-providing, peace-giving treasure that every heart needs is a Person. He is extremely personal, yet can be shared with another person. He gives strength in times of stress, yet offers comfort in times of sadness. He grants us wisdom when we are confused, yet corrects us when we are wrong. He provides help when we are needy, and his help will never end. For he guides us continually and stays "closer than a brother" (Prov. 18:24).

He gives commands to be carried out, but promises wonderful rewards for obedience. At times he allows loss, distress, and pain, but he always gives us something better. He does not impose himself upon us, but patiently waits for us to invite him into our lives. He does not force us to do his will, but is painfully disappointed when we do the wrong thing. He desires that we love him because he first loved us, but he allows us a free will to choose him or reject him. He wants to take care of us, but refuses to force himself upon us. His greatest desire is to be our Father, but he will not intrude. If we want what he wants—a loving, caring Father-child relationship with him—we must accept his offer. He is too considerate to force it. If we have not received Christ as Savior and Lord, he is waiting for us to become his child. Of course, as you have surmised, he must be a personal God.

This personal, intimate relationship with God through his Son Jesus Christ is the most important thing in life. This is the "something" young people are yearning for: "the meaning in life," "something to count on," "something to bring comfort when everything seems to be falling apart." It's all there.

Do you have it? If you don't, seek help from a minister or a Christian friend.

The second requirement is that children identify with their parents so that they can accept and incorporate their values.

As you recall, if teenagers do not feel loved and accepted, they have real difficulty identifying with their parents and tend to react to parental guidance with anger, resentment, and hostility. They view each parental request (or command) as an imposition and learn to resist it. In severe cases, teenagers learn to consider each parental request with such resentment that their total orientation to parental authority (and eventually to all authority, including God's) is to do the opposite of what is expected. When this degree of alienation occurs, it's nearly impossible for parents to give their moral and ethical value systems to their teenagers.

In order for teens to identify with their parents, relate closely with them, and be able to accept their standards, they must feel genuinely loved and accepted by their parents. To lead a teen to the close relationship with God that they themselves possess, parents must make sure that a child feels unconditionally loved, a topic we have previously discussed. Teenagers who do not feel unconditionally loved by their parents will find it extremely difficult to feel loved by God.

Religious Training

A very important thing to know about teenagers is how their memory operates. Remember that teenagers are children emotionally and are much more emotional than cognitive. They therefore retain feelings much more readily than facts. Children can remember how they felt in a particular situation much more easily than they can remember the details of what went on. For example, children or teenagers in a Sunday school class will remember exactly how they felt long after they forget what was said or taught.

So, in some ways, whether a child's experience was pleasant or unpleasant is much more important than the details of what a teacher taught. By pleasant I do not mean that a teacher need cater to children's desire for fun and frolic. I mean that the teacher should treat children with respect, kindness, and concern, and make them feel good about themselves. A caring teacher will not criticize, humiliate, or otherwise put down a child.

If religious training is a degrading or boring experience for young people, they are likely to reject even the best teaching, especially when morality and ethics are involved. It's from this type of situation that a teenager develops a bias against religious matters and tends to consider church people as hypocrites. This attitude is difficult to rectify and can continue with a person for a lifetime.

On the other hand, if the learning experience is a pleasant one, a teenager's memories of religious things will be pleasant and can then be incorporated into his or her personality. Emotionality and spirituality are not entirely separate entities. One is quite related to and dependent upon the other. For this reason, if parents want to help a teenager spiritually, they must care for the child emotionally. Because a child remembers feelings much more easily than facts, there must be a series of pleasant memories within which to accumulate the facts—especially spiritual facts.

The Wait-and-Choose Approach

Now let's examine a popular misconception that goes something like this: "I want my child to learn to make his own decisions after he is exposed to things. He shouldn't feel he has to believe what I believe. I want him to learn about different religions and philosophies; then when he has grown up, he can make his own decision."

This parent is either copping out or is grossly ignorant of the world we live in. A child brought up in this manner is to be pitied. Without continual guidance and clarification in ethical, moral, and spiritual matters, this child will become increasingly confused about the world. There are reasonable answers to many of life's conflicts and seeming contradictions. One of the finest gifts parents can give a teen is a clear understanding of the world and its confusing problems. Without this stable base of knowledge and understanding, is it any wonder many children cry to their parents, "Why didn't you give me a meaning for all this? What's it all about?"

Another reason this wait-and-choose approach to spirituality is grossly negligent is that more and more organizations and cults offer destructive, enslaving, and false answers to life's questions. These people would like nothing better than to find a person who was brought up in a seemingly broad-minded way. This teen is easy prey for any group offering concrete answers, no matter how false or enslaving.

It's amazing to me how some parents can spend thousands of dollars and go to any length of political manipulation to make sure their children are well prepared educationally. Yet, for the most important preparation of all, for life's spiritual battles and finding real meaning in life, children are left to fend for themselves and made easy prey to unhealthy influences.

Prepare Your Teenager Spiritually

How do parents prepare their teenagers spiritually? Organized religious instruction and activities are extremely important to a developing teenager. However, nothing influences a teenager more than the home and what the teen is exposed to there. Parents need to be actively involved in a teenager's spiritual growth. They cannot afford to leave it to others, even superb church youth workers.

1. Parents must teach their teenager spiritual concerns. They must teach not only spiritual facts, but how to apply them in everyday life. And this isn't easy. It's quite simple to give a teenager basic Scriptural facts, such as who different Bible persons were and what they did. But that is not what we are after ultimately. Help your teen understand what meaning biblical characters and principles have personally. You can do this only at somewhat of a sacrifice, as with focused attention. You must be willing to spend time alone with your teenager in order to provide for emotional needs as well as spiritual needs.

2. Parents must share their own spiritual experiences. With the factual knowledge gained from church, Sunday school, and home, a teenager only has the raw material with which to grow spiritually. The teen must learn to use this knowledge effectively and accurately to become a mature person spiritually. To do this, a teenager needs the experience of walking with God daily and learning to rely on him personally.

The best way to help a teen with this is to share your own spiritual life with him. As your teenager matures, gradually increase your sharing about how you yourself love God, walk with him, rely on him, seek his guidance and help, thank him for his love, care, gifts, and answered prayer.

Share these things with your teenager as they happen, not afterward. Only in this way can a teen get "on-the-job" training. Sharing past experiences is simply giving additional factual information, not letting teenagers learn for themselves through experience. There is a lot of truth in the old statement, "Experience is the best teacher." Let your teen share in yours. The more a teenager learns to trust God, the stronger the teen will become.

Teenagers need to learn how God meets all personal and family needs, including financial. They need to know what their parents are praying for. For example, they need to know when you are praying for the needs of others. When appropriate, they should know of problems for which you are asking God's help. Don't forget to keep them informed about how God is working in your life and how he is using you to minister to someone. And, of course, teenagers should certainly know you are praying for them and for their particular needs.

3. Parents should be examples of forgiveness. Teach your teenager by example how to forgive and how to find forgiveness, both from God and people. Do this first of all by forgiving others. Next, when you make a mistake that hurts your teenager, admit the mistake, apologize, and ask forgiveness. I cannot overstress how important this is. So many people today have problems with guilt. They cannot forgive or they cannot feel forgiven. What can be more miserable? But the fortunate person who has learned how to forgive those who offend and who is able to ask and receive forgiveness demonstrates a mark of mental health.

4. Parents must train teenagers how to handle anger maturely. As we discussed in chapter 7, it's normal to a certain extent for a teen to handle anger in passive-aggressive ways. This antiauthority attitude and motivation, if not checked and redirected, will cause a teenager to choose a value system (including spiritual values) incompatible and usually opposite of parents. Normal passive-aggressive tendencies should be resolved and disappear around the ages of 16 or 17. As this happens, a teen's basic attitude toward legitimate authority (especially parents) will be positive. Then as the young person chooses his or her life's ethical and spiritual value system, usually between the ages of 18 and 25, he or she will be able to use rational, logical, clear reasoning in doing so and not be influenced by self-defeating, passive-aggressive anger. Therefore, parents must be diligent in teaching teenagers how to handle anger.

Balcony People

My former pastor, Moncrief Jordan, told me a story about a friend of his. And because it has bearing on how we deal with our teenagers, I want to tell it to you. Pastor Jordan's friend said that when he was trying to deal with his own tendencies toward discouragement and despair, he would let his "balcony people" speak to his "cellar voices."

The cellar voices in all of us come from the basements of our lives. Sometimes they are impulses and urges we normally associate with the animal kingdom—rash temper, boiling anger, and vindictive feelings.

But the cellar voices go beyond emotional or physical reactions. They proceed from the dark side of ourselves—a dark side that most folks rarely see. The cellar is where our scenarios of hate, greed, pride, lust, and destruction are formed. And woe to that person who does not recognize the potency of this area!

The cellar voices also come from those around us who, because of low self-esteem, guilt, frustration, or pent-up hostility, cut us down, telling us how bad the world is and how bad we are. If we let them, these cellar voices can lead us to despair and hopelessness.

But fortunately, Pastor Jordan's friend also told him about balcony people. These are the people, living and dead, who have lifted us with their love, faith, hope, and courage.

We all need balcony people who show us that we can live above the petty and discordant levels of life. That we do not have to wallow in negativism and despair. That we do not have to let our inner conflicts wreak havoc in life. That we can live victoriously. The balcony people speak to us both with their talk and their walk.

Some of the balcony people in Scripture are beautifully summarized for us in Hebrews 11, in a roll call of people who proved that faith is workable, and that life can have meaning and purpose at any time in history.

Most of us can learn from our own experiences. But it takes a wise person to learn from the experiences of others. It's our privilege to let our balcony people save us from unnecessary mistakes and conflicts, and to lift us up in hope.

Perhaps we should consider writing our own "eleventh chapter of Hebrews," listing our own balcony people. Do you realize we have more balcony people to draw from than any previous people in history?

From our list, there ought to be a select few balcony people who are living today and with whom we can bare our hearts and souls from time to time. These are people we utterly trust and admire and to whom we can reveal our dark sides, knowing we will be loved and prayed for. That is part of what the church of Christ is all about.

Our teenagers need balcony people to give them hope. They are hearing more than enough cellar voices. We must be balcony people to our precious youth. But we must work at it—we do not have to be spreaders of gloom and doom. Teenagers are very sensitive to pessimism, especially from their parents. We do not have to buy into the despair of our day. Faith in our God and in ourselves—have you read Hebrews 11 yet? No? Hurry up! It brings a hope that cannot be destroyed.

God gives us hope. Hope is not wishful thinking. Hope is the knowledge that the wonderful promises of God are true. God has made many promises to us. Read them for yourselves. Start with Romans 8:28: "And we know that all that happens to us is working for our good if we love God and are fitting into his plans" (TLB).

Or how about Jeremiah 29:11: "For I know the plans I have for you, says the Lord. They are plans for good and not for evil, to give you a future and a hope" (TLB).

Or consider Isaiah 41:10: "Fear not, for I am with you; be not dismayed, for I am your God! I will strengthen you, yes, I will help you; yes, I will uphold you with My vindicating right hand" (MLB).

Or look at Psalm 34:19: "Many are the afflictions of the righteous; but out of them all the LORD delivers him" (MLB).

Christian Hope

We must have recovery of hope in our land! Our young people need hope to face an uncertain future. I know the situation does not look good right now. But, as in generations past, if we give our youth what they need to face the future, they will be prepared and will do well. We must give them confidence, courage, moral strength, and a sense of responsibility. We cannot give them these priceless assets without hope—the sure knowledge that God exists, that he loves us, and that his promises are true.

Moncrief Jordan told me of a man he visited regularly. This man had many physical ailments, and eventually both of his legs had to be amputated. Pastor Jordan thought that this would surely break his joyful and optimistic view of life. But it didn't.

The man would still swing himself with a trapeze device from his bed to a wheelchair and roll himself down to the parlor in the very depressing nursing home where he lived. There he would play the piano and sing until he had many others singing with him. During his last years, he was the channel of hope and joy to many people.

Christian hope does not depend on what the world does to us. It depends on what we do in the world as we live in response to God's great love for us.

Fellow parents, let's be encouragers, dispensers of hope that teenagers so desperately need—"balcony people," as some call those who watch over others to lovingly help them along in life. It's difficult to be a balcony person, but I guarantee you that it really pays off, for it's like giving water to a drought-parched earth. And best of all, we are giving our teenagers what they need to become balcony people themselves.

By nature, I am not as much a balcony person as my wife, Pat, is. And through the years, it has been pure joy to see my daughter and sons follow in their mother's footsteps. They are balcony persons also. How I admire that and try to become more that way!

Let's grow together, fellow parents. By working at it every day, we will gradually become more and more like Christ—the ultimate balcony Person.

12

The Older Adolescent

As adolescents near the time of normal separation from home, they still need their parents to help them make that precarious crossing into adulthood. Contrary to what many parents assume, this crossing does not happen instantaneously through a high school graduation or a move out of the house. The transition into adulthood should be a gradual weaning process for which both parents and teenager prepare.

You first prepare for this change by making sure your teenager has learned to lead an independent life. There may have been "practice runs" at living away from home for periods of time as children were growing up, such as summer camp experiences and visits with relatives. Now you need to increase your teenagers' self-sufficiency by making sure they can actually take care of themselves. Can they do their own laundry? Prepare balanced meals? Handle all the other necessities for independent living?

These needs are usually overlooked, especially with boys. It isn't unusual for a boy or a girl living away from home for the first time to fix the same unhealthy, starchy meal over and over to the point of developing vitamin deficiencies and becoming susceptible to illness.

By the time your adolescents becomes independent, they should be able to handle their own finances. This means budgeting income and balancing a checkbook. Such items may seem like common sense, trivial matters, but many adults still cannot balance a checkbook, much less discipline themselves to save money.

It takes time to train teenagers to manage their affairs; it never just happens. I am amazed, for example, at how many college students cannot even get up in the morning to arrive to class on time. Self-discipline is best learned before leaving home. Seldom is it sufficiently learned later.

Lifelong habits are usually shaped during later adolescence. Although most of a teenager's adult traits or characteristics have been partly formed, they are usually still changeable. Both parent and teenager should make use of this time to enhance favorable characteristics and hopefully modify less desirable ones.

Goal-Orientation

One of the most important aspects of a teenager's personality is the teen's degree of goal-orientation. No one, and especially a teenager, is perfectly balanced in this area of being goal-oriented. Some people are too goal-oriented, putting almost all their personal resources into reaching what they want—good grades, a college degree, money—to the exclusion of other equally important matters such as fun, relaxation, and personal relationships. A person who is too goal-oriented tends to be perfectionistic, judgmental, rigid in thinking, opinionated, tense, and worried. This person also takes things too seriously and personally. Many people who are reading this book will fit into this category, just as I do.

It's fine to be goal-oriented and conscientious. But people who are excessively so will tend to find life a drudgery with little pleasure. They will also increasingly tend toward depression as they become older, especially during the middle years. They have made reaching for goals their meaning to life. So when they reach those goals, they wonder what meaning is left. If they do not reach their goals, they likewise see little meaning. If your older adolescent has these traits, you can be of tremendous help by teaching how to find significance in pleasant hobbies and other means of relaxation, and

especially to learn the immense value of friends and personal relationships. It's still relatively easy for an older adolescent to change.
However, the older a person grows, the more difficult it is to
change. The more perfectionistic and goal-oriented an adult is, the
more apt he or she is to become dull, depressed, rigid, and unpleasant in old age.

I am reminded of two people who present stark contrasts in this
area. Once I saw a 67-year-old man who had been a hard worker,
devoting almost all of his energy to his job. He allowed little time
for family, fostered few friendships, and was quite a perfectionist.
His life was fairly satisfying until retirement. Without his goal
(hard work), he lost most of his meaning in life and rapidly became
profoundly depressed. When I saw him, he stared straight ahead,
as though he were in a catatonic trance. He could hardly move and
just sat motionless, day after day, until his family brought him for
treatment.

The exact opposite is our dear next door neighbor, a widow. She
has been a woman of accomplishment and still is involved in many
projects. Yet she has always loved people and fostered close relationships. People feel wonderful just being around her.

What a difference! The man has been too perfectionistic and
goal-oriented; our neighbor has achieved a wonderful balance. It is
important to remember that their personal characteristics were
present in late adolescence and simply intensified over the years.

The more a teenager sees the meaning and value of human relationships, the more that teen will develop into a pleasant, congen-
ial person who can roll with life's punches without crippling
depression. The key is balance. You want your older adolescent to
have the essential degree of goal-orientation to enable him or her
to have a life of satisfying accomplishments. But you also want
your teen to be person-oriented so that he or she can have truly
meaningful personal relationships, as a spouse, parent, and friend.

My precious daughter Carey and I had long discussions along
these lines before she went away to college. I emphasized the
importance of friendships acquired in high school and college.
These are truly special friendships that should be kept alive over the
years, if at all possible. I recommended that she keep a notebook

with the names and addresses of every meaningful friend she makes so that she can keep in touch with them over the years.

Although we form close friendships after our school days, there is something special about high school and college friends. These are the people we can call on years later and almost always find an instant rapport. It is as though the conversation simply picks up where it left off—back in the "good old days." Appreciation for friends is especially important for the older adolescent who is so goal-oriented that he or she tends to devalue friendships.

However, your adolescent may be just the opposite. The orientation may be to relax, have fun, enjoy life, and to delay responsibility as long as possible. As common sense will tell you, these traits should be identified and worked on from very early adolescence.

You may have a teenager who is capable of making good grades but who is having so much fun in activities and with friends that he or she doesn't give proper time and effort to academics. It is appropriate to handle this problem directly, if your child is not strongly passive-aggressive. If you are not dealing with an anger problem, you can help your teenager become more balanced in approach to responsibility. If you have done your job as a parent, making sure your teenager feels unconditionally loved, you have every right and responsibility to expect your teenager to take the proper amount of responsibility and become properly goal-oriented.

This reminds me of an experience with our David when he was 13. He was capable of making good grades and did so—until the beginning of the seventh grade when he became so engrossed in football and friends that his report card showed all Cs. Knowing this was far below his ability and seeing his strong drift toward fun and frolic and excessive peer interaction, Pat and I knew we must make some changes. We set up a system calling for each of David's teachers to send home a weekly grade over the six-week grading period. We told David each time he brought home a grade below a B, there would be no sports for the coming week. We established and enforced guidelines for good study habits. Not only did the next report card reveal all As, but David's whole attitude toward academics had changed. He really felt good about his success and no longer needed coaxing from us.

Occasionally, an older adolescent will have a negative academic attitude as high school graduation approaches. This often happens to a teen who has had previous learning disabilities or perceptual problems; and it may create conflict with the parents who have high future academic expectations. Consider each situation separately. I've seen many instances of this kind resolved by encouraging the teen to take off a year or two to work or assume military duty. Often this course will give the adolescent the time and experience he or she needs to mature, settle down, and become appropriately goal-oriented, both vocationally and socially.

Preparation for the Real World

One of the most difficult dilemmas that parents face today is preparing young people to handle the real world with its alcohol and other drugs, sexual license, decaying spiritual values, and general attitude of "me-ism" or selfishness. This is a difficult subject even to write about because it's so controversial. I believe it's a cruel blunder to completely isolate children and teenagers from the world as it really is, but I have seen many parents do this. Eventually, of course, we must let our sons and daughters go. If our young people have not learned how to deal with these pressures while living at home, how can they cope with real life when they are on their own?

While your teenager lives at home under its haven of safety and guidance, he or she needs some exposure to these problem areas in a controlled way. Of course, I don't mean encouragement or permission to "live it up" for the experience. I mean training your teenager how to cope with real life and setting privileges based on trust, consequences of behavior, and appropriateness of the social occasion. These privileges should be controlled to progress in such a way that you can help your teenager handle different encounters as they arrive. Teenagers need to be well trained on how to handle most of life's situations. Of course, this does not mean that they are to participate in unhealthy activities. Rather, they should learn how to handle themselves maturely and determine to keep themselves pure and uncontaminated by the unhealthy aspects of today's society. To achieve such maturity will take time, preparation, training, conviction, and self-control on your part.

One of the most serious mistakes you can make is to assume that school, church, or other organizations can or will handle this part of your child's development for you. The parent has the greatest effect on the teenager, especially regarding values and lifestyle. Schools and churches can help, but without the primary involvement of the parent, a teenager will not usually do well. Sending a teen off to college without preparation for life is copping out on parental responsibility. I have seen many adolescents who seem to behave well at home go wild as soon as they are away from their parents' control. They haven't learned the self-control necessary to handle independence and freedom.

To help prevent this catastrophe, work with teenagers as they become independent. You want teenagers to realize that you are working with and not against them, toward their independence and freedom. In doing so, you will want to be careful to follow the guidelines of trust vs. consequences. During the few months before they leave home, you can gradually make teenagers' privileges similar to those they will have where they are going to live—a college dormitory or apartment. You'll be training your teenager to cope by using self-control and taking responsibility when there is little or no supervision.

Such training is hard on parents. After years of carefully training and supervising our children, we must learn to let them go, and this is a frightening experience. But it is so much easier and so much more constructive to do it at home in a carefully planned and gradual way, working as a team with our teenagers to accomplish it. This means gradually removing as many rules as possible to give teenagers a few weeks or months of experience with the independence appropriate for an adolescent ready to leave home. We have to be careful here. If we have done our job in training our teenagers, they will handle themselves well.

However, there are a few very common conflicts that often arise and could be disturbing to the rest of the family—such as coming in at late hours and upsetting other family members. Or being inconsiderate in not letting the household know where he or she will be, especially at mealtimes. Or failing to carry out an expected chore or errand. Or not showing up where and when expected. If such behavior persists, parents need to revert to making privileges contingent on trust and consequences of behavior since the teen is not ready for full assumption of responsibility.

Security

Although our adolescents are nearing adulthood, their emotional needs have changed little since childhood. Even at this stage, they need to know that we genuinely love them, that we are available, and that we will help them in any way we can—for their own good. As long as they feel we truly care for them, we can continue to have constructive influence in helping them achieve independence.

One problem for many parents at this point is the old enemy—anger. Some parents who handled anger well when their adolescents were younger have a real problem handling it at this critical point. We must remember that this final separation is difficult for our teens. It's a long weaning process during which we must remain available to offer support and help. Have you ever watched a mother bird push her youngster out of the nest when that time has come? I recently watched several nests of swallows where the mothers were performing this difficult task. Some of the young birds flew with no problems. Some had difficulty learning to fly, and mother and father were available to help where needed. Then it happened. One young bird frantically tried to fly but fell through the air. The sickening thud told us the tragedy—it was not ready for departure and the parents were not available to help in this last phase.

Even after young people leave home, they still need us. They need to know we are there, available, and ready to help when needed. In chapter 9, I mentioned a visit that Pat and I had with Carey's friends at college during their freshman year. All of these fine young people were happy in school and with their new friends. But they all had the same complaint—they seldom heard from their parents. Not enough calls, letters, or visits.

When we later related this to Carey, she admitted she felt the same way, which surprised me. But after thinking it over and remembering my first days away from home, I began to understand. The weaning from a good parent-child relationship is slow and often painful. After that weekend, Pat and I made it a ritual to call Carey every Sunday night to make sure she knew we were thinking about her, praying for her, and ready to help where we could.

Another characteristic about departing young ones is their need for everything to remain the same—just the way they left it. This helps the young person feel secure. It's a good idea to keep as many things as possible the same, especially rooms and personal possessions. Older teenagers may feel terribly hurt if their rooms are turned over to younger brothers or sisters. And don't be too quick to sell your house and move to smaller quarters. I've heard several teenagers say, "I sure hope my parents never sell our house. I want always to be able to go back home."

However, the most important anchor of security a teen leaves behind is the marital relationship of his or her parents. One of the most devastating things that can happen to adolescents soon after leaving home is the separation or divorce of their parents. It's as though the foundations of their whole world are crumbling. Yet, it's amazing how many parents actually plan to "stay together for the sake of the kids, but as soon as they leave home, we're getting a divorce."

This is extraordinarily unwise. Not only is a teen's basic foundation crushed, but the blow occurs at the very time when he or she most needs support—a time when the teen is desperately trying to adjust to a new life, new friends, etc. In most cases, a young person will be burdened with heavy guilt. Regardless of how unreasonable it may sound, a young person feels that he is somehow responsible, either for the bad marriage or for the divorce. If a divorce is inevitable, it's far better that it take place long enough before adolescents leave home that they can work through the natural feelings of loss and grief with help of parents, friends, and minister before they takes on the difficult task of leaving home for the first time.

I know one young man, John, who believed that his parents were happy in their marriage when he left for college. Within three months they were divorced. The mother remarried soon afterward and sold the family house. John seldom went home because it was so depressing for him. His base of security was destroyed. You can imagine what this did to his sense of well being.

Another important factor as children leave is that they stay involved with sources of security, stability, and growth. One of these is the church. It's important not only to attend church regularly with children and teenagers, but to do all we can to make the church experience pleasant for them. A good youth group is critical, especially in the teen years. As children move to college or work, we need to encourage them to become involved in church and Christian activities.

Spouse Selection

One of our priorities as parents was to make sure each of our children could identify the qualities that are desirable in a future spouse. It's not easy for a teenager to identify traits within a peer that indicate the ability to be a good spouse or parent. Because dating is a somewhat artificial situation, a young person often doesn't have much to go on other than how "good" he or she feels with that person. Of course, simply depending on such superficial feelings can be disastrous. Regularly, I counsel young people who have made that tragic mistake. They have depended on their feelings to decide whether to become involved or marry rather than considering other far more important factors.

One of the first things Pat and I taught Carey about this matter was to look at the character of a boy, as well as to consider the feelings he produced in her. We explained to her that the best indicator of how he will treat his wife after marriage is the way he presently treats persons whom he is not required to treat with consideration—those who are elderly, unpleasant, or helpless. We told her to observe how he treated people in service jobs, such as waiters and waitresses.

A third consideration, and the one Carey really latched on to, was to see how he treated and related to children, especially small ones. For you see, Carey had two younger brothers, providing a perfect litmus. Before we gave her these insights, she used to make sure David and Dale were out of sight before a date arrived. After our discussion, Carey would ask David and Dale to answer the door and talk with her date while she "got ready." It was interesting to watch Carey observe her date from a hidden place, to see how he did with her brothers. Our discussion truly helped Carey gain priceless insight into the boys she dated.

Carey certainly applied the valuable insights she learned from Pat and me. She married a few years ago. Her husband, Chris, is one of the finest young men Pat and I have known. We truly thank the Lord for Chris. He and Carey, by the way, have presented Pat and me with a wonderful granddaughter, Cami.

Another characteristic of a person who will be a good spouse or parent is the ability to reason. This is critical in marital and parent-child relationships; to be a reasonable person, one must be able to reason. A person who can reason usually has the ability to come to an agreement or compromise in family conflicts. In other words, the person can argue from a point of view but is able and willing to be proven wrong or to compromise and to come to a mutual understanding with spouse or child. On the other hand, a person who cannot reason will almost invariably be unreasonable. He or she will be unable to argue—that is, explain a viewpoint in a conflict—and will probably demand his or her own way.

If you're looking for them, you can identify these traits after a short period of time, especially during a situation in which the person is angry. A person who never gets angry should be suspect. He or she could possibly be passive-aggressive or may not have the resources to develop a real emotional attachment to anyone. Either of these character types is difficult to live with. However, we must say that there are caring persons who simply are so low-keyed that they seldom are provoked to anger. I envy them. They are rare.

Another indicator, which is extremely important but difficult to discern, is a person's ability to manage ambivalence. Ambivalence is having opposite feelings toward the same person. Although ambivalence is difficult to detect, I think the best way to do so is to observe a person's tolerance of different kinds of people. For example, consider the person who has strong and uncompromising opinions about everything. To this person, there is no gray area, no room for compromise about anything. He or she sees people as all right or all wrong, all good or all bad. This person cannot see that there is good and bad, pleasant and unpleasant, in everyone. We all have ambivalent feelings. Handling them well, on a conscious level, is an indicator of maturity. (See chapter 2 of *How to Really Love Your Child* for a deeper discussion of ambivalence.)

Another good way to determine what kind of spouse or parent a person will be is to watch how the person gets along with his or her own parents, brothers, sisters, grandparents, other relatives, and long-time friends. This is an excellent indication of how the person will treat his spouse and children in the future.

One problem in letting feelings have too much influence on one's choice of a spouse is that a young person will fail to ascertain the true character of a prospective mate. Character is not easy to define nor easy to discover in a person. Character is a person's underlying attitude toward himself or herself in relation to others and his or her pattern of behavior.

Most people naturally put their "best foot forward" to make a good impression, especially during courtship. Eventually, however, their true character will emerge in all its good and bad aspects. It's crucial for a person to know all he or she can about a prospective spouse's character. Unfortunately, it takes a long time for a person's true character to emerge—especially the negative component. One of the most important truths I've tried to pass on to my children is that you must know a person well for at least two years before you understand his or her true character. This is one critical reason why the divorce rate is so high. Most people marry primarily on the basis of feeling, not understanding the character of the spouse, and hence marry too soon.

Be Optimistic

We've talked about some painful things. But we've also talked about how we can and should be optimistic and hopeful about our teenagers and their future. Yes, many of our youth have serious problems, some even severe. But many are doing beautifully and are a real encouragement to me. Many times we have had the college students from our church come to our home for a get-together. What an uplifting time it was for me, with these warm, wholesome, mature, vivacious, and lovable young people. It reaffirmed for me that our efforts are worthwhile.

This book on teenagers was written expressly for you by another parent. My strongest desire was to see my children grow into strong, healthy, happy, and independent adults—and they did, thank God. I desire the same for your teenager. Some of the material in these chapters may be difficult to fully grasp on the first reading. I strongly suggest that you now reread the book and let the material come together for you in your particular circumstances. We need to be reminded continually how to really love our teenagers.